"Deeply per ... .cui,
Shirin Amani's beautiful immigrant's memoir
would touch the heart of anybody who has ever
been an outsider, with a sense of wonderment,
irony, longing and humour. A moving and
fascinating read about displacement,
integration, solidarity and friendship."
Daphna Baram, author of
Disenchantment, The Guardian and Israel

"This is an exceptionally candid, sensitive and lively
account of an immigrant's experience in an alien society,
one which both reaches out to welcome her but which,
at the same time, finds it difficult to accommodate her
sense of difference and remoteness. The beautiful Persian
stories at the end of her chapters have been skilfully used
to define her sense of otherness, and the sense of them as
a refuge and consolation is extremely touching."

"I really hope she will be able to write more and
elaborate on her experience and those of others like
her. A very rewarding read altogether – we need to hear
voices like this one."
**Jonathan Keates, writer, biographer, novelist
and former chairman of the *Venice in Peril Fund***

Once Upon a Time
in
Uppsala

Shirin Amani Azari

The Book Guild Ltd

First published in Great Britain in 2023 by
The Book Guild Ltd
Unit E2 Airfield Business Park,
Harrison Road, Market Harborough,
Leicestershire. LE16 7UL
Tel: 0116 2792299
www.bookguild.co.uk
Email: info@bookguild.co.uk
Twitter: @bookguild

Typeset in 11pt Minion Pro

Printed and bound in the UK by TJ Books LTD, Padstow, Cornwall

ISBN 978 191535 2880

British Library Cataloguing in Publication Data.
A catalogue record for this book is available from the British Library.

ACKNOWLEDGMENTS

To my daughter Maya, my mother's other grandchildren and those who enjoy learning about life through tales. With many thanks to my husband Paiam, for his encouragement through his patience and for believing in me when I didn't. A special thanks to Mr James Loader for being with me right from the start. Finally thanks to all those who supported me without knowing it.

In the memory of my beloved mother, grandmother and all the great women who shape our lives in magical ways in the short time that we are given to spend with them.

In tribute to Mahsa Amini and all the Iranians who risk their lives in hope for democracy in Iran.

Woman – Life – Freedom

ONE

The cold is like no cold that I have experienced before; it is indescribable. The chilled breeze finds its way to your flesh through all the layers that you carry for protection against it. The days are short and dark. The lack of traffic and pollution adds to the homesickness.

The desire to leave the flat in the morning wears off as soon as we face the layers of snow that have been laid out overnight. The tasteless and oddly shaped vegetables make dinners feel like an obligation. The lack of communication and facial expressions between people on public transports or in the streets makes you cry for human attention and contact.

The ultimate peace and calm are nerve-racking. The royal treatment of pets is amusing. The facilities for the older generation are unfamiliar. The blond hair colour of the blue-eyed race is overwhelming. The distance between people while they communicate with each other is offensive. The lack of an attentive ear, the lack of empathy and physical contact, feels isolating.

The number of Volvos in town makes the non-Volvo cars stand out. The dress code of being covered from head to toe for protection from the cold, rather than one forced by the government, is ironic. The law and order is untouchable. No fear for life, safety or other security issues is sensed in this country of ice, which no war has touched for more than one hundred years.

'It has come to my attention that you and your children have missed your appointments at the Office for Social Security since your arrival. They have raised their concern and I have been appointed to discuss this matter with you,' Katarina, the social worker, said with a serious face, standing in the middle of the lounge of our new flat.

'It's too cold to leave the house,' my brother Shahin said, while my mother and I smiled.

'*Det finns inget dåligt väder, det finns bara dåliga kläder*, as we say in Sweden.' Katarina half-smiled. 'It means that there is no bad weather, only bad clothes or inappropriate clothes for the weather,' she continued.

We only smiled as it would have been rude to talk back, we thought.

'Look, this is the Swedish weather; it will not get any better until April or May. If you are waiting for better weather before you step out of the flat, you'll have to wait a long time,' she said, still half-smiling. 'Sweden can get below twenty-five degrees, during winter, and that's what we call a good winter. You cannot focus on the weather to find a daily routine,' she insisted.

We looked at each other tearfully.

'Don't worry,' I whispered to my mum in Farsi. 'We aren't staying here for long, only until the war is over. We will be going home soon.'

'It is rude to speak in a language that others don't understand,' Katarina said, looking at me. Not receiving the response that she was expecting, she stood up and, before she closed the door behind her, she said, 'Welcome to Sweden.'

The long journey had not only left us exhausted but also forced us to the realisation of how far we were from our country. Trying to create contact with our loved ones back home soon proved to be harder than we thought.

Communication with them required a day trip, taking the weather, bus schedule and facilities available into consideration to reach the telecommunication centre before it closed. The phone number in question had to be given to the lady at the cashier. She would then tell you which telephone to stand by while she tried to make contact for you. Waiting anxiously by the phone stand, praying that the communication line would be clear and that Maman Bozourg or Meme would pick up the phone, made us realise how starved we felt of their love and attention.

This attempt to communicate with our loved ones would not be more than once a week and would last no more than ten minutes, split between the three of us. Sometimes the signal would break up in the middle of our conversation, owing to the poor reception in Iran. Sitting in the corner of the office, trying to put each of our conversations together in order to make sense of the well-being of our relatives, made us cry for the circumstances that we felt trapped in.

Happy were the days when we made our trips to the post office. The efforts to make the trip felt minimal. A snowstorm could not stop us. Clutching the notification letter from our local post office, we would gladly queue up for our parcel from back home. The excitement of opening the parcels was sometimes overwhelming. The guessing game between Shahin and me was amusing and added more flavour to the excitement. The parcels usually contained dried herbs, rare spices, pistachios, Zereshk berries and, on rare occasions, sweaters knitted by Meme to keep us warm. The evening would start with opening the packages of salted, freshly roasted pistachios carrying the aroma from home, watching the television with the two choices of the Swedish channel SverigeTV1 and SverigeTV2, while the scent of *ghormeh sabzi*, made from freshly dried herbs, would fill the air and finally make room for Iran in our Swedish flat.

It was on one of those trips to the post office that we met Auntie Sima. She seemed full of life and joyful as she volunteered to help us with small matters at the post office. She told us that she had lived in Sweden for four years. *That's an eternity*, I thought.

'Days pass so quickly,' she said.

'If you have fun, they say,' I replied. It turned out that she had had no fun in the four years that she lived in Sweden. She had been unhappy in her relationship since her husband had converted to Christianity. She had a daughter whom her husband was not the least interested in, and she felt very lonely, as we did.

Auntie Sima was kind-hearted and introduced us to the local church, to the local library and to the small Iranian community living in Uppsala, but most importantly she introduced us the Swedish Festivity events, such as *Fettis dagen*, when all the shops and bakeries were filled with *semlor*. *Semlor* – Lenten buns – have a layer of marzipan and whipped cream inside, with the hat powdered in icing sugar; they taste heavenly in a bowl of hot milk or on their own with a glass of cold milk. The fasting period before Easter is two weeks and the tradition is that on the last day of the fasting, you feast on *semlor*. We were just grateful to the bakeries for their *semlor*, no matter the story behind them.

Easter celebrations started the Thursday before Good Friday. This Thursday is called *Skärtorsdag*, and the children would dress up as witches, and go around knocking on doors for candy. Good Friday was spent indoors mourning Jesus's death by watching films of His life, from His birth until His death, for three long hours. It must be the only time of the year that both Swedish TV channels showed the same programme so that no one would, God forbid, miss Jesus's life story. Easter Sunday would be celebrated with friends and relatives. Being invited to a Swedish family celebration felt like torture. We would struggle with the language, trying to make a conversation, keeping it alive by smiling, laughing, giggling at the right sentences. It required you to use all of your senses and a lot of body language to make sense. Mostly it looked as if you were playing a game of charades. Then, all sweaty and out of breath, you would sit down to have the Easter food that had been prepared for you, which would involve boiled eggs cut in half and decorated with marinated fish and pickled onions. *Sill* (Atlantic herring) was served from jars in different sauces, and there was always a dish of *Jansson's Frestelse* – Jansson's Temptation, a traditional dish with layers of onions, anchovies, potatoes and cream. Looking at the Easter table, trying to find something that you would be able to wash down with the fizzy Easter drink, *Påsk Must*, was always a struggle. The dessert was the best part of the evening and would make up for the ordeal that you had been through earlier. An Easter meal with Swedish friends was such hard work that we volunteered at an organisation run by one of Mum's friends, which served *Påsk* lunch, Easter lunch. Bibi Andersson described the work done by this organisation as a good deed, and always said that we made her proud.

We learned that the Eurovision Song Contest was one of the highlights of the year for the Swedes, who would gather around a television that Saturday evening to have a proper countdown with family or, more usually, friends, eating crisps and snacks while discussing the worst and best performances. Voting was a must; you had to support the neighbouring countries as it was against the rules to vote for your own. The whole evening passed in excitement, with everyone agreeing to disagree on the winning number. Then there were the headlines in the daily papers, the morning after, '*Rätt låt vann* (Right song won)' or '*Fel låt vann* (Wrong song won)'. It was the only time in the year that the editor of each paper legally had the right to express an opinion in print about a certain issue. The discussions about the songs continued for weeks, if not longer, and started again a couple of months before the next Eurovision contest. It was such an alien feeling to watch a nation so involved in an issue that was not related to politics.

Olof Palme was the Prime Minister at the time and very popular amongst people in Sweden. Owing to his activities for peace and his attempt to create peaceful contact between countries, he was one of the most renowned and popular Swedish Prime Ministers. His phrases were known and quoted by most communities, and one that was repeated on a daily basis was 'There are two things you cannot trust in Sweden: Swedish women and Swedish weather'. It was a sad day, when his murder was announced. He was considered kind and generous to the asylum seekers, refugees and immigrants. His death was mourned nationwide, if not worldwide. The Kurdish, Chilean and Iranian communities grieved in their own cultural ways, holding different ceremonies and gatherings in his memory.

That was the only time I felt even slightly close to Swedish politics. The subject in Sweden felt like a taboo, even when it was taught in school. Teachers were not supposed to reveal their political sympathies and the subject more or less turned into history, as you studied the historical aspect of politics. It could also turn into geography, when you studied the geographical input, influence and involvement of politics, but many times the lesson became a philosophy session where you answered a question with another question. The democracy within the politics felt agonising. The freedom of thought and speech felt tortuous, coming from a land where you are told what to think, what to believe, what to say and how to be. It took a while before you allowed yourself to express your newly found thoughts and beliefs.

Uppsala was the capital city of Sweden in the sixteenth century. It is a university city designed well for students. Being the fourth biggest city in Sweden, Uppsala charmed us with its old area, its cathedral – the Domkyrka – and its astonishing castle. The River Fyris – *Fyrisån* – was the jewel of the city. On Saturdays the farmers covered both sides of the bridge of *Fyrisån* with their delicious organic seasonal fruits, berries and vegetables. The ice-cream kiosk nearby, selling the famous Swedish *mjuk glass* – soft ice cream – would bring a smile to your face no matter the weather conditions. The full length of *Fyrisån* was lined with cute restaurants, cafés and people happily meeting there for fun, but the most well-known event of the year in the university city of Uppsala was *Sista April*, or Walpurgis Eve, the last day of April when Student Day was celebrated. The day began with an early morning champagne breakfast for the graduate students, followed by the annual boat race by the students in the river. It was loud, joyful and exciting. Lunch was usually brought in picnic baskets to the city park if the weather allowed.

Our first experience of *Sista April* was covered in snow and did not live up to the expectations. The horror of walking through the snow and not knowing when the summer would appear was unbearable. The river had frozen so the race had been cancelled. The students drank limitlessly to celebrate, which seemed like drowning their sorrows. It was cold, snowy and windy, and as we walked home from the city, we admired the determination of many to celebrate Student Day, despite the weather conditions. '*Det finns inget dåligt väder, bara dåliga kläder*,' Shahin and I rhymed, and giggled, as we skipped home.

Bellman Skolan was the nearest school to our new home that had accepted us to start already in May. Shahin and I excitedly watched other children make the trip to *Bellman Skolan* every morning, knowing that we would join them one day soon. The journey to school was very different to what we were used to. The children walked or cycled to school, sometimes accompanied by their parents but mostly on their own. We observed in detail in order to learn the behaviour and the routine of the trips, so that we would fall into normality on our first day at the school. We found the stories arising from the journey to school fascinating and we couldn't wait to take part in them. Boys following girls, girls playing hard to get, older siblings leading, helping, bullying, arguing, fighting the younger siblings and vice versa. Flowers were gathered, and berries such as gooseberries, black, white and red currants, were picked in the local communal garden, to be shared with your walking companion as soon as you reached your apartment. The local kiosk offered sweets, snacks and their famous hamburgers and hotdogs to be purchased, but we soon learned about *Lördagsgodis*, Saturday sweets, which meant that Swedish children were only allowed sweets on Saturdays. They would choose a bag full of pick-and-mix and then spend the rest of the day going through it. The Saturday treat meant a lot to the nation's children and parents. It was used as a bribe or threat the whole week. It worked wonders on behaviour.

Our local supermarket, Vivo, could satisfy the weekly needs but had only a few aisles. Freely renting a movie at Vivo felt strangely liberating.

The youth club provided baking sessions, table tennis, games and guitar lessons for young people. To freely listen to music, play instruments and dance felt like a guilty pleasure at first, but it soon turned to a normal daily routine.

We could count up to a hundred, could say some phrases in Swedish, but didn't feel confident enough to take part and be involved in the projects at the youth club. However, we did feel ready to start school.

And the start of school was the start to all of our adventures. It could be described as the wardrobe of Narnia: the new, exciting and scary world of the Swedes.

TWO

Bellman Skolan was the school, Ulla and Ruth were the teachers and there were six of us in the class, who eagerly and desperately wanted to learn Swedish as a foreign language. Ulla had shiny white bobbed hair and the bluest eyes I had ever seen, with a smile permanently fixed on her kind face. She walked quickly with rather small steps, head down to speed up the process, but spoke slowly in order to make sense. She didn't mind speaking English at times when it was needed. Ulla was the grandmother figure whom we all so much missed from back home. We all sat with fascination and listened to her stories, and lessons felt amusing. She had the ability to make the most boring sentence sound fascinating and exciting to listen to.

Ruth was the strict version, with not so much grey hair, being younger. She was taller and grey-eyed, and only smiled when she felt like it. Being selected for Ruth's class rather than Ulla's felt like a curse, even though the Iranian *Tarof*, a traditional form of civility, prevented us from complaining. So we joined her sessions with a smile on our faces, expecting a smile back. Her classes weren't as amusing as Ulla's. Ruth plainly had a mission to complete and it was completed only when we had finished our session with her.

There were six of us who had joined more or less at the same time and could speak as little Swedish as each other. Shahin and I were accompanied by another Iranian boy, Farshid; an Eritrean boy, Ted; a Kurdish boy, Murat, from Turkey; and another Kurd from Turkey, a girl called Turkan.

Farshid was one year older than me, dark-skinned with curly black hair. Murat was one year younger than me, fair-skinned with light brown eyes and hair. Both were very macho and were eager to learn Swedish in order to chase the Swedish girls at school. Ted was a happy, chirpy guy who was a girl's best friend. He usually spent a lot of time with us, being philosophical about girls' issues.

Turkan was dark-skinned, shy, eager to help others and very affectionate. She endeared herself to me, like everyone else, the first time I saw her, and thirty years later, with thirty thousand miles between us, she is still my very good friend.

The school was on one level, with only five grades. Each grade had two classes and each class had fifteen children. It had a gym hall and a music room but no dining hall. We had to eat at a different school which was within walking distance but altogether scary, as we had to dine with the older children. No gum or sweets were allowed in school during school hours, and we did not wear uniforms. There were stands outside school where you could park your bicycle and lock it for safety. The non-uniform policy allowed the freedom to be creative in your fashion sense, but it also created a lot of pressure, especially for me, who wanted to enjoy the freedom. The 'No sweets, ice cream or gum' policy within school hours was hard to obey, especially as the shops and kiosks nearby offered all that could be purchased to ease the sugar cravings and increase our energy level.

Our gym teacher, Nisse, was a tall, middle-aged man who was kind, encouraging and full of energy. However, gym sessions were the worst hours of our lives. I hated gymnastics, hated climbing, balancing, jumping over the benches, hated volleyball, basketball, football, hockey, but mostly I hated playing *brännboll*, which was a Swedish outdoor sport very similar to baseball. I dreaded the sunny days before the summer break when we had to play *brännboll* outdoors. I didn't understand the game and couldn't relate to it in any way. Looking back, I feel sorry for Nisse, waiting enthusiastically for us to arrive with sour pale faces, dreading the worse, ready to vomit out of fear and embarrassment, and not wanting to move about at all.

The sports that I was interested in, such as ping pong and badminton, we didn't spend enough time playing, I felt. We had to be taught to swim, so every week we made our way to the city swimming hall and in six weeks I had learned to swim one hundred metres. It was dreadful leaving the swimming hall with half-dried hair to make our way back.

'Don't touch your hair, it may break if it freezes.'

'Same goes for your ears, Amani,' I used always to hear as I waited for the bus to take us back to school.

We had to learn to ice skate and to ski, at least cross-country skiing. It just didn't make sense to me to spend time in the cold, trying to find pleasure in the name of sport. 'You'll get warm as soon as you move about,' I used

12

to hear. Perhaps I didn't move about as much as I should have, but it certainly didn't make me any warmer.

The facilities were available for all types of sports and activities that you could imagine, both in school and after school, but in my case the will was not there to commit to learning an utterly foreign sport. It was as if you would be a traitor, learning a Swedish sport and enjoying it.

Our Swedish classmates in Year 5 were awkward. After our Swedish lessons we joined them for sports, music, art and maths lessons. They could no more relate to us than we could relate to them. Thank God for Turkan in my class, I used to say! I was far ahead in Maths and therefore not liked by my awkward Swedish classmates. They must have felt the same about me: too dark, too short, too loud, too chatty, too cocky and too eager to learn.

Our Year 5 teacher's name was Ylva. She was kind but firm. She was fair and dealt with the issues amongst the children almost immediately. She also encouraged and supported our abilities and potentials. One of Ylva's hobbies was travelling to different places and she was very fond of Greece. She compared us to the children living in Greece with their culture, and that's how she could relate to us. We were grateful for that.

The boys in the class at that age were showing interest in the girls and the girls were receptive to this. It was very unusual to us to be so open about sexual and emotional feelings at the age of twelve or thirteen. By the time we joined the fifth-year class for a few sessions, the boys and girls were already paired up. '*Jag ar ihop med Tomas* (I am with Tomas),' we used to hear from Anna, or '*Jag vill vara ihop med Martin* (I want to be with Martin),' Helena would say. There were few who considered being with the opposite sex meant only in the sense of friendship.

I had found my lifetime friend and I was happy. Turkan called me 'sister' from day one. Maybe in Kurdish culture you are meant to call your friend a sibling, but I took that title seriously and obeyed the rules. On the first day of school we discovered that we were neighbours too. She lived on the first floor and we lived on the second floor in the same apartment block. We used to call each other, if needed, from our balconies. She lived with one of her elder sisters and one of her elder brothers, as well as their mum, in a two-bedroom flat. Her mum, her sister and Turkan herself were great cooks. The aroma from downstairs, especially if it was a sunny day and we had left the balcony doors open, was tormenting. We would always get a plateful of food to taste from their kitchen. We were grateful for the plate, which was more than a tasting portion – sometimes the whole evening meal was provided by *Anne*. That's what we called Turkan's mum: *Anne*, mother in Turkish.

The Cicek family soon proved to be kind and generous neighbours who brought us comfort, love and warmth in the cold and lonely days of our new life in the unfamiliar country. The days seemed to become lighter even in the dark months, warmer in the cold; you could sense the birds chirping, the flowers blooming and the ice melting, and in that spring of 1985 a family of seven was created.

Food platters were exchanged between the first and the second floor, the tea pot was always on the brew in both apartments in case of a pop-in, the balcony doors were left open so the families could communicate, the cycling trips to and from school were made together, the gooseberry

14

and currant pickings outside our building were made on a daily basis, the laundry room in the basement was occupied at the same time by the two families, so that we could spend as much time as possible together. During the evening the Turkish videos held our attention, and whilst playing them on our video, we would drink tea, eat sweets and munch on nuts and savouries from back home. Even if we didn't understand the language of the movie, we would read between the lines and cry when the others cried and laugh when they laughed. Turkan and her family did not speak English, but somehow Turkan and I always (in some mysterious way) spoke Swedish to each other.

THREE

'Shirin, Shirin!'

I rushed to the balcony when I heard Turkan cry but didn't need to reply; instead I looked down. There, lying on a beach towel underneath our apartment, with her back towards the sun, was a naked woman. The looks between Turkan and me spoke a thousand words. What was she *doing*? Obviously, neither of us had the answer, and we were certainly too embarrassed to ask our mothers. We decided to ask Ulla as soon as we got to school. We cycled fast but carefully. We laughed as soon as the other one laughed, asking each other if the woman would cover herself when she turned over, which made us burst out laughing all over again.

Grinning and holding back our laughter, we found Ulla in the classroom, preparing her morning session.

'You'll never believe what we just witnessed this morning,' I started.

Ulla looked up, with her glasses slipping down her nose so we could have eye contact with her sky-blue eyes. She smiled and waited patiently until we had finished shrieking with laughter.

We took it in turns to finish each other's sentences, trying to make some sense.

She finally took off her glasses and said, 'Have I understood this correctly? Please correct me if I haven't... so there was a lady sunbathing on a beach towel in a field outside your building?'

'Sunbathing? She was naked! Completely naked! No tops or bottoms!' I tried to convince her of the shock we had had that morning.

'I hear you, but I don't understand what the issue is,' Ulla tried again. 'A lady was seizing the opportunity to sunbathe in the morning sun, and gain some vitamin D.'

'If you could call her a lady.' I giggled. 'Ladies do not sunbathe naked,' I continued.

'Listen, you two,' Ulla said. 'The summers are very short in this country and we seize every opportunity, especially in the summertime, and this is how we sunbathe: *naked.*'

'Oh, dear Lord, so men as well as women, sorry... I mean, gentlemen as well as ladies... sunbathe naked in the summer in Sweden?' I said, with a hint of sarcasm.

'Well, my dears, after spending a few winters in Sweden, I am sure that you will sunbathe naked too,' she said, putting her glasses back on and returning to her paperwork.

Then and there Turkan and I made a pact to never sunbathe naked, no matter how many cold winters we would spend in Sweden.

We spent the whole morning remembering and visualising the woman, and laughing about the matter.

After lunch, we joined Ylva's class for mathematics. Turkan and I were always joined at the hips when we entered the classroom. It felt cold, strange, unwelcoming and different. We were still smiling as we went to our places, until the cold looks we received made us stop.

17

We sat at our benches, with our heads down as we tried to avoid the stares of a bunch of frozen blonds, who looked at us as if we were aliens from a different planet. We did an hour of maths – additions, divisions, subtractions and problem-solving – until Turkan asked me for help.

I turned to her paper and had a look at the question but found it so easy that I must have sniggered. I turned back to my paper again. When I looked up I saw my friend watching me with her eyes full of tears. It broke my heart to see her so upset. The tears rolled down her face and I felt powerless. I couldn't find any words to express my regret for my behaviour, so I leaned towards her, dried her tears and kissed her on the cheek to comfort her.

With that one kiss on her cheek, all hell broke loose. The whole class started to whisper, pointing fingers, making kissing noises and loudly laughing.

'*Tyst!* (Quiet!)' Ylva said firmly, not knowing what was going on and not really caring.

I knew that we were safe for now, even if I could hear occasional laughter and a kissing noise here and there, but we had to face the world and these students after school. I had to take the bull by the horns and put a stop to this nonsense.

So, all pumped up with adrenaline, I stood up, filled with guilt for having caused my friend yet another misfortune, and said, 'Please allow me a couple of minutes of your class's precious time, Ms Ylva.'

She nodded, sensing that it was an important matter, half-smiling at my polite way of speaking.

'This morning we witnessed a bare woman sunbathing outside our building on a beach towel, miles away from any beach, stocking up on vitamin D apparently, and we found that extremely strange, although it is normal to you. Kissing someone's cheek in our culture is not only a form of comfort but it is also the way we greet each other when we say hello and goodbye. That's not only normal to us – it is impolite if you do not observe the custom. If we can accept that lying naked in the sun is normal to you, then you can have the decency not to make fun of our harmless way of greeting and comforting.'

I noticed halfway through my speech that Ylva had started to translate my words into Swedish. After I had finished, she said, 'Thank you, Shirin, you may sit down now… I don't want to hear about this matter again,' she continued. We all knew that she meant it and it was never mentioned again.

I felt very sad for the gradual loss of our culture but filled with pride at the same time. As Ulla said later in her class before we ended our day at school, it was a '*Kultur krock*' ('culture clash')! It was a new term to learn but to understand the meaning of it cost us dearly, and this was only the beginning.

In bed that night I thought of Maman Bozourg (my maternal grandmother) and her wise words, and what she would say to me before I fell asleep and dreamt: *Yeki Bood, Yeki Nabood…* Once upon a time there was…

Once upon a time, there lived a powerful king who had the most beautiful, elegant and wise daughter, called Homa. Princes from near, far and beyond had been waiting and longing for her hand in marriage.

The beautiful princess was kind to all living creatures and was very much loved amongst her people.

Every morning the Princess would start her morning routine by sitting at the window of her bedroom, feeding the birds and entertaining them with her singing voice.

Each of the birds, that were forty in number, never less, never more, would show its gratitude for such love and attention by chirping in time to the songs.

One morning, while Homa was fully engaged with her morning routine, one of the birds, with magnificent blue feathers, snatched a golden bracelet off her wrist and flew away with its fellows.

Princess Homa took this to heart and fell ill when the birds did not return the following morning. Not knowing what had caused such heartache, the King called for the most skilled physician in the land.

After a thorough examination and much consideration, he suggested to the King that he should build a public bath in the city centre for people to use, in exchange for a story, as a distraction to the Princess to forget her grief.

Nima, a hard-working young boy who found the idea of treating his widowed mother to a bath appealing, was searching for a story to tell, when he noticed a trail of camels approaching. They seemed to be carrying sacks of gold. He hid behind a tree and then crept quietly after them.

On went the camels, steadily, at a leisurely pace, until they reached the golden gate of a garden. The gate opened by itself and the camels stepped through. As the gold-sacks were being unloaded, Nima sneaked into the garden.

Nima felt as if he had died and entered paradise, amongst all the heavenly flowers, trees and bushes, with their divine colours, delightful shapes and sizes, and charming scents.

The beauty of it all made Nima dizzy so he hurried into the house and hid behind the door of a room, which looked like a dining room. The table in the middle of the room was covered with a feast fit for a king.

When Nima didn't think that it could get any more dreamlike than it already was, a flock of birds flew in through the window. Amongst them was a charismatic blue-feathered bird, which suddenly turned into a tall and most handsome prince.

The Prince took a bracelet out of his pocket and laid it on his prayer mat, and stood in prayer. Strong, tall and decisive, he raised his hands and demanded to be heard by his God.

'Oh, almighty Lord, please let the owner of this bracelet be mine,' he cried.

Nima felt for the Prince, and was relieved, as he understood that he could help the Prince with his great wish.

On the way home, he thought about his story and with great confidence asked for an audience with the Princess.

Princess Homa looked pale, heartbroken and melancholy.

Nima started his story from the beginning of what he had experienced.

When he reached the part where the blue-feathered bird, accompanied by forty others, had flown in, Princess Homa fainted. Her team of maids tried to bring her back to life by splashing rose water on her face, and when she opened her eyes again, she asked Nima to continue his story in detail, word for word. She listened carefully to the story and asked him to take her to the house.

The following day, all set and ready for an adventure, hidden behind the trees, waiting patiently for the camels to arrive, Nima asked Princess Homa for a promise to look after his mother in case anything happened to him.

When together they sneaked into the garden, Princess Homa realised that Nima's description of the garden did not do it justice. She was mesmerised by the enchantment of it and let her imagination swirl freely around and explore it all, until Nima whispered, 'Come with me!'

Inside the house, they hid behind the wall of the dining room where the table was set as grandly as the day before. Not long after, the window to the room blew open and forty white birds, accompanied by the blue-feathered bird, fluttered in. The forty birds each sat on forty chairs around the table, leaving one seat at the head for the guest of honour. One by one the white birds turned into beautiful, tall young girls, before the blue-feathered bird was transformed into the charming prince.

Princess Homa gasped!

After they had feasted the Prince was left on his own. He looked at the bracelet around his wrist and sighed.

Preparing for his prayer, he laid the bracelet on top of his prayer mat and prayed fervently again for the owner of the bracelet to be his.

Princess Homa could hardly contain her excitement, but Nima signalled to her to wait.

'I, Prince Arsalan, who have so little power and have been cursed to live as a bird with forty other birds from a young age to this day, have yet again fallen into the curse of love with Princess Homa." He raised his hands to his God and prayed for liberation.

Princess Homa wept. Prince Arsalan heard her cries, lifted his head, opened his eyes and saw that Princess Homa felt the same way as he did.

While they sobbed in each other's arms, Nima kept watch and worked out a cunning plan to break the curse.

Prince Arsalan explained that because of a feud between his father and the King's brother, a spell was put on him by his uncle's most trusted minister, in cooperation with a witch. The birds were head over heels in love with the Prince and would rather die than leave him. They were also cursed, and had been sworn to kill anyone getting close to Arsalan. The spell on the Prince would only be broken if the birds left him.

Princess Homa sighed in despair.

'Would the birds follow you if you flew far away?' asked Nima.

'They would fly with me, no matter how far I flew!' the Prince replied.

'You look as if you have a potential solution,' Homa said to Nima, hopefully.

'I might,' said Nima with a sparkle in his eye.

For the next forty days, Prince Arsalan flew far away and beyond, from dawn to beyond sunset, followed by his forty companions. In the meantime Nima kept busy in the garden digging a tunnel from one end to the other, while Princess Homa waited patiently at her palace. Prince Arsalan had warned them both about the jealous and possessive nature of the birds.

Then one morning Prince Arsalan woke up earlier than usual, took a warm bath, dressed himself in new clothes and prayed to his God, asking for Princess Homa's hand in marriage. He then set off with his bird fellows, flying to a new destination farther than ever before.

That morning Nima also woke earlier than usual, devoutly said his morning prayers and shared the loaf left from the night before with his mother for breakfast. He kissed his mother, as though it were the last time that they would see each other, and set off to the garden.

Princess Homa too woke up in the early hours of the morning, and prayed to her God. She asked for the blessing of marriage to her prince. After her prayer she left the palace to be with him on his return.

At sunset as planned, Nima waited in the garden at the end of the tunnel he had dug, with a flaming torch in his hand. Meanwhile Homa waited patiently indoors, keeping watch from the window, until she glimpsed the blue bird in the red sky. She closed her eyes and prayed.

She prayed for a good outcome, to finally be with her prince, for the spell to be broken, for Nima to be safe during the process and for the souls of the forty birds who had also fallen under the spell of the wicked witch.

When she opened her eyes, keeping her hands and teeth clenched together, she saw her handsome blue bird flying into the tunnel, followed by forty white birds, like a thundercloud. He seemed faster than the rest, probably because they were tired after flying so far that day. Nima stood guard with the fiery torch at hand and as soon as he glimpsed Arsalan coming out of the darkness he set fire to the big hole at the entrance to the tunnel. The forty white birds turned into black dust and smoke, which came out of the tunnel with a cry. To Homa's surprise, forty snakes then crawled out and crept into the ground, shrieking.

Nima was celebrated as a hero and was rewarded greatly. The Prince and Princess lived happily ever after.

And Nima's mother had a very well-deserved bath at the palace!

FOUR

The days grew longer and warmer; it was unbelievable that such a frozen land would finally melt and the sun would bother to shine on this part of the world.

'It could have been worse, we could have ended up in Iceland or Greenland,' Mum used to say, just to comfort me when I complained about the weather.

'We are going back home soon anyway,' I answered. I found that reply extremely soothing, while also knowing deep down that there was a big question mark hanging over whether we would ever go back. The war was getting worse. Iraqi troops had got closer to Tehran, people in Tehran lived in constant fear and were evacuating the city on a weekly basis, and mostly choosing to live in the countryside.

The news on Swedish TV about Iran was minimal. We only had two channels to rely on and it seemed that Iran was not part of the world, and that there was no war in that part of the world. Telecommunications with our families were limited, not only because of the cost but also because of government regulations in Iran, where, it was believed, all the conversations were monitored, checked and recorded.

We relied on the letters from my father, Dayee (maternal uncle) and Auntie Shokooh for inside information. Reading between the lines we gathered that things were not looking good. Auntie Sima's father had made a pact with God (a *Nazr*), that if the war ended, he would walk to the City of Yazd from Tehran. Auntie Sima often told us this, with pride. She wished her father to see that day, but I always wondered how he could walk ten thousand miles.

'He will probably lose his life on the way, which would be so ironic having survived the war and then dying in paying his thanks to God for having his wish come true,' I used to say to my mum.

'Keep your thoughts to yourself,' my mum would reply. '*Nazrs* offer people hope. They believe in *Nazrs* as they believe that God will hear them and respond in a positive way. One needs to believe, hope and live in hope.'

'One also has to make a reasonable pact with God, surely. I cannot make a pact with God, that if the war ends and Iran is safe, I will climb the Himalayas?' I said, with one eyebrow raised.

'That will be between you and your God,' she said. 'Now go and find someone your age to play with. Where is Turkan? I have not seen her today,' she said, clearly wanting to distract me.

I took my weekly pocket money and went downstairs to find Turkan, and soon we were on our bikes, cycling into the city of Uppsala. For a long time I had been wanting to buy Michael Jackson's latest album, and today felt just like the day. We cycled in the sun, enjoying the late spring breeze, raced and laughed, and made it just in time to the Tempo shop (which later was renamed Åhlens). On Saturdays the shops would close at 2pm. We only had a couple of hours to browse, buy the album, come home and listen to it in peace, take it all in and learn to sing and dance to it. Turkan didn't understand my excitement over all this, but, being a loyal friend and my partner in crime, she happily joined in and shared the excitement.

Once inside Tempo, we found the music department, which was just as you entered the shop. I approached the assistant and asked for Michael Jackson's latest album.

'Sorry, I don't understand who you mean,' she said firmly.

I looked at Turkan, thinking that the woman must be kidding me.

I tried again, naming the previous album, *Thriller*, but she shook her head. In desperation I started to sing the song and then acted the dance moves on the shop floor. Turkan started laughing but I was determined to show the woman who I meant; I could not believe that they did not know the legendary Michael Jackson in this part of the world, as we did even in Iran, where all his music, videos, photos and posters were banned.

Suddenly, she shouted, 'Meekaiil Yaksoon!', as if we were playing a game of charades.

'Who?' I asked.

'Meekaiil Yaksoon,' she said, while she took out his album cassette, feeling proud of herself for figuring out who I meant. I looked at the cassette sadly. 'His name is Michael Jackson,' I whispered. 'Everyone knows that. He is a legend. It would be as if I were to call you "Catherine" instead of "Katarina", even if you are not a legend,' I continued in a low voice while paying.

'How do you know my name?' she asked.

'It's on your badge,' I said, as we left the store.

'What's wrong, Shirin?' Turkan asked, while we were licking our *mjuk glass*, ice creams.

'I miss everything and everyone from back home. I cannot adjust. I find it too hard, my friend,' I said, licking around the cone to stop the melted ice cream running down.

'Perhaps you need to lower your expectations?' she said, and licked her own ice cream.

'What do you mean?'

'I mean you need to see beauty in all the new, and stop comparing it with all that are you are used to and all that you have had and seen,' she said, searching for a tissue in her pockets.

'Wise words! I am lucky to have you as a friend. I could have kissed you, but…' We both laughed out loud.

Full of laughter, yummy ice cream and stocked up with vitamin D, we were making our way to our parked bicycles when we hear the alarm of the store Tempo going. I had not heard the shop alarm before, so I was confused by the sound. Not long after this we saw a young girl running out of the store, yelling in Farsi, 'Save yourselves! Seek shelter, seek protection!'

We watched while she was caught by the security guards and taken back to the store. She had her head down and you could see that she was in tears.

'We have to go in with her,' I said.

'Are you mad? They will think that we are partners in crime with her,' Turkan said.

'Perhaps, but we know that we are not! By the way, I don't even believe that she is guilty of anything, especially not shoplifting. She said to save yourselves and seek shelter in Farsi,' I argued firmly.

'Perhaps she was carrying a bomb,' Turkan said, pulling me towards our bicycles.

'What if she wasn't? What if she needs support and help? Cyrus the Great once said that there are no crying voices worse than a child crying for the loss of their mother, a lover crying for a separation and an innocent pleading in tears for a crime they have not committed,' I said, feeling like a soldier of Cyrus the Great, spreading his message, with my head held high.

'Look, Shirin, you are my friend, and I would go to hell and back for you, but I don't think that I can go in there,' Turkan said, shaking her head in regret, ignoring my speech.

'You don't have to, my friend,' I reassured her.

I quickened my pace as I saw the men vanishing into the store with the girl, and when I was halfway there I smiled, when I noticed Turkan shadowing me.

We knocked on the door of the security office where we had seen them go. A tall blond security guard opened the door.

It was a long afternoon, with the police officer, security guards, tears, headaches and apologies until her foster parents finally arrived. It came out that while Sedigheh had been in the store looking through the make-up she heard the alarm. Memories made her believe that it was the alarm for an Iraqi attack, and she reacted on impulse. She ran out seeking shelter and was mistaken for a shoplifter. They believed her once her foster parents arrived and, as they had not found anything on her, they gave her a long lecture about how she should not run out of the store when the alarm went off. This would only distract the security guards from finding the real shoplifter, the security guard explained, without showing any sympathy for the behaviour that she had learned.

She was taken by her foster parents to Knivsta (a city near Uppsala), where she lived with her foster family, as she was underage. I never saw her again.

'See, things could've been worse,' said Turkan. 'You could have been here on your own, without your mum and Shahin, living in Knivsta, and we would never have met and become friends.'

'Have you taken clever pills today?' I asked, knowing how right my friend was. 'One thing is for sure, though,' I continued.

'What's that?' Turkan asked, having had enough of my sarcastic attitude for one day.

'That you would follow me to hell and back,' I yelled out while cycling ahead, knowing that I would do the same for her.

FIVE

Sundays still felt unusual as it was another day of the weekend, while we were only used to one. The weekend in Iran is only one day – Friday. Sundays in Sweden felt like a forced day of rest. All the shops were closed and not many people spent time outdoors, especially in winter. Summertime offered a few options, such as picnicking in the park or making a trip to the lake to picnic, bathe and sunbathe.

Shahin and I woke up one sunny Sunday and made Mum breakfast in bed. She needed cheering up, we felt. She had been unhappy for a while but never spoke of her sadness. She kept it all to herself and we let her do so.

She appreciated the breakfast but didn't seem to enjoy it as much as we had hoped she would. She dropped crumbs on the bed, she kept spilling the tea and her boiled egg fell on the floor and cracked open. Finally she suggested we ate breakfast together at the kitchen table.

'Isn't it better to eat together instead of you two watching me while I'm eating?' she said.

'What would you like to do today?' I asked Mum. 'We'll do whatever you like to do today, it's your day today!' I added cheerfully. She gave me a look that spoke a thousand words. I realised that I was powerless to give her what she wanted. She wanted to have her life back with her husband; she wanted a big hug and wise words from her own mum.

I looked down, trying to stop my tears from rolling down my cheeks.

'Anybody home?' we heard through the letterbox.

'It's Gulbahar,' I said, and jumped out of my chair, as if I had heard an angel calling.

Gulbahar was Turkan's older sister. She was beautiful, full of energy and joy, and a dedicated smoker and tea drinker.

She walked in with a plate full of *lahmacun*, Turkish mini pizzas.

'Who died?' she asked, laughing. We laughed with her. She opened the balcony door to let in some fresh air. 'It's a wonderful day: sunny and warm. It won't last long, we'd better enjoy it as much as we can,' she said. 'Look, the naked lady is already out there,' she continued, pointing out of the window.

We laughed so hard that we became tearful. Turkan called from her balcony and we asked her join us. She came, along with her mum, and we put the kettle on and had the most magnificent brunch in our small kitchen, with the Turkish pizzas and freshly brewed tea, talking about the past, the present and the future in five different languages: Farsi, Kurdish, Turkish, Swedish and English. My mum had become fluent in Turkish (the Turkish that they speak in Turkey, not Azari Turkish), I understood Turkish and Kurdish, while Turkan had become really good at Farsi. Moreover, our Swedish was progressing rapidly. So our communication skills were hard at work to make the conversation enjoyable.

While we were deciding what to do or where to go for the rest of the afternoon, we heard 'Sarkhosh' from the balcony. The Ciceks (Turkan's family), who had lived in that building before we moved in, had named our drunken neighbour *Sarkhosh*, which means 'drunkard' in Turkish.

Urban was his real name – at least that's what we heard his wife call him from the balcony, when he had gone out to walk the dog. Sometimes she would call for him for hours, sitting on the balcony – 'Urban! Urban! Urban!' – until he returned.

We would hear him swear at her as soon as he got close to the building: '*Jävla kärring. Jävla forbannade kärring. Stick for i helvete! Lämna mig ifred!*'

For a while we thought that his wife's name was Kärringen, until we figured out that *kärring* meant old bitch in Swedish.

The couple lived with their dog on the third floor above us. They did not work and were alcoholics, waking up at midday and abusing one another, as well as their dog, until Urban left the building. Then the wife would call him back for hours on end until he'd return.

We suffered in silence but had also learned to live with it. We never took the lift, as we couldn't risk being in the same lift as them. We would always listen in the hallway to avoid walking on the stairs with them, and close the windows and the balcony door as soon as we heard them. The thumping, the swearing and beatings we would still hear, but at least we felt safer behind closed doors.

'It sounds really bad this time,' Shahin said.

We looked at each other for support and listened carefully for clues as to how bad it could be.

The balcony door remained open to satisfy our curiosity.

'*Din förbannade kärring! Jag är så trött pa dig, Jag ska döda dig* (You damn bitch, I am so tired of you, I'll kill you),' we heard Urban say. He kept on repeating it, until we heard someone or something being dragged across the kitchen floor to the balcony. The thumping and swearing continued. I ran across to hug my mum, and soon Shahin joined us too.

All eyes were fixed on the balcony. We heard someone being pushed against the balcony grids over and over again.

'How do we stop him? He is going to kill her!' I said.

'Nothing is going to happen.'

'It's the dog he is messing with.'

'It's not the wife, surely?' I heard everyone say.

It was hard to judge from the noises, whether it was the dog or the wife, for as one howled, the other screamed, cried and pleaded, while Urban swore.

Mum, Shahin, Turkan and I hugged each other tightly, while Gulbahar bravely moved towards the balcony to research further, and in that split second we saw Kärringen fall helplessly.

She landed face down on the grass. We all ran on to the balcony and looked over it. It was a horrifying sight. A sight that no child should ever have to witness! I had been through a revolution and a war but had never seen a sight as horrific as this, I thought. Escaping war and death suddenly felt ridiculously ironic.

Kärringen was lying on the grass motionless, while Sarkhosh yelled out loudly and safely from his balcony, 'If anybody calls the police, I will kill them too. Let her die! Let her die!' we heard him roar, over and over again.

We were shaking in fear, fear for our lives, for our safety, but mostly shaking for our powerlessness.

We stood above her on our balcony, while my mum dialled the emergency code for the police.

We all testified to what we had seen. The officers were gentle and promised us safety. We watched as the ambulance took her away. Before they left, we were informed that she was still alive.

The police officers escorted Urban to the police station. The dog was taken to a home for pets. We were all shaking from the experience but laughed when Urban returned home weeks later, soon followed by the Kärringen in a wheelchair, with a broken neck. All went back to normal for the couple when their dog came back as well, except that now, Kärringen would sit on the balcony, in her wheelchair and motionless, yelling, 'Urban! Urban!' until Urban came back from his walk.

The story was in the paper the following day, and when we told Ulla about our experience she showed us the article. She was concerned for us, and we still shook when we told her the story.

That evening we slept in Mum's bed for a long time, talking about the past, grandmothers and their wisdom. Finally, when the clock struck ten, I moved to my bed and dreamt of a story that took me to a faraway land, a warmer, safer place, a place that was familiar and good.

Yeki bood, yeki nabood... Once upon a time...

Once upon a time there lived at the foot of the Alborz Mountains a happy couple with their newborn son, Bahram. But not long before Bahram's first birthday, his father passed away.

His mother worked hard, and single-handedly brought up her son, cared, fed and educated him until he grew into a handsome young man.

When Bahram turned eighteen, his mother sat him down and said that his father had left some money to be given to him at the age of eighteen, to do business with and invest, to make a good living for himself and his mother.

Bahram kissed his mother on the forehead and took one hundred silver coins of the money and the following morning set off to the market to double it.

On the way to the market, he saw some boys tormenting a cat, beating it with a bat, throwing water over it, kicking it and spitting on it.

'What has this poor cat done to you to deserve this kind of harshness?' asked Bahman, with a crack in his voice.

'You want to save it? It will cost you one hundred silver coins.' They laughed.

Bahram was taken aback by their demand but felt that if he could offer them the money to save the cat's life, he was morally obliged to do so.

He gave them all his money. Just before the cat ran for its life, it whispered to Bahman, 'This kindness of yours will never be forgotten.'

When he told his mother at home about his act of kindness, she said, with a mixture of pride and disappointment in her voice, yet determinedly, that his family should come first.

The next day Bahram was given yet another one hundred silver coins and, with a kiss on his forehead from his mother, he set off to the market, hoping to set up a business and earn a living.

At the market, as he was focusing on the sales of the day, he heard a terrible howling from a dog that was being beaten cruelly while being dragged by a thorny lead.

His natural instinct led him to beg the bullies to release the dog, but he was put in the same situation as the day before. He had to bribe them with one hundred silver coins for the life of the dog.

His mother was not happy with his decision, although she was slightly relieved at having raised such a wise and kind-hearted son.

On the third day, using her most determined tone of voice and explaining the situation better and more clearly than before, she gave her son the remaining one hundred silver coins. With her kiss on his forehead, and hoping to make a profit, Bahram set out for the market.

At the market, after some research and discoveries, he decided to invest his money in nuts, and as he was negotiating with the dealer, he heard a group of men arguing. Getting involved, he realised that the argument was over a box.

Knowing that he would regret his question, he asked what was in the box. Inside he saw a beautifully coloured snake. Its silky skin was covered in patterns and it had the most vulnerable eyes he had ever seen. As soon as he laid eyes on it, he swore that he would do anything to save it.

The negotiations led to a hundred silver coins changing hands, and the snake was released outside the town, far away from civilisation, with Bahram as a witness.

At sunset, Bahram sat under a fig tree and, with a big sigh, wished for enlightenment. At that point, the beautiful snake appeared at his feet.

'I owe my life to you, and so does my father, the great Chief of Snakes, the ruler of all snakes,' hissed the grateful snake. 'He will celebrate you as a hero of his clan.'

Bahram, whose curiosity was awakened by such news, accompanied his new friend to meet its father.

On the way Bahram told the snake all about his troubles and how he had lost his and his mother's investment, as well as her trust in his ability to make an income. The snake listened patiently, admired Bahram's courage, kindness and honesty, and before they reached the gates of the Chief of Snakes' palace, it said, 'When my father, the Chief of Snakes, asks you what he can offer you in return for saving his only son from being burned alive, ask for the Ring of Solomon.'

The Chief of Snakes was delighted by the safe return of his beloved son and honoured Bahram with a feast, the very same evening.

'Bahram, what can I do to return the favour of you saving my first-born?' asked the Chief of Snakes when the moment was appropriate.

'I ask for nothing, but if you insist, I would like to ask for the Ring of Solomon.'

The Chief of Snakes' face turned bright red but he kept calm.

'That ring has been passed from Solomon to me for generations in a very delicate and cautious manner. I have sworn an oath to keep it safe from ignorance, unkindness and cowardice. Even though today you have been proved to be kind-hearted, brave and wise, I still hesitate!'

After a long pause, he lifted his head again and continued: 'Is there anything else I can do for you or anything else I can give you?'

Bahram's face fell.

After a long silence that felt like eternity, the Chief of Snakes opened the precious chest that many of his loyal companions had been lying on, protecting it from evil, and took out the actual Ring of Solomon, Son of David.

'This is not just an ordinary ring. With this ring, you can control and possess all the power you may need in favouring others, good or bad. My son recognises you to be genuinely wise, brave and kind enough to be worthy of this possession. I trust his judgement. He is willing to give up his inheritance and offer it as a favour to the saviour of his life. My concern is that your own life might be endangered by the possession of this ring, and worse, if it falls into the hands of the unknown.'

Bahram nodded in agreement.

In a very powerful yet beautiful setting, with many witnesses and guardians of the ring, the oath was made, the prayers were said and the ring was handed gracefully to its new owner.

Bahram headed home cheerfully to test the power of the ring, remembering all the promises that he had made to keep it and himself safe. He followed the instruction of wearing it on his middle finger. He ran his hand over it, and a genie appeared from its stone in a puff of smoke, and was soon very much alive and ready to assist.

Bahram immediately asked for a mansion to live in with servants, an easy life with prosperity. His mother was as pleased as she could be with this trade.

One day as Bahram was going past the King's palace, he noticed the Princess walking in the garden. When she saw him, she giggled.

Bahram became so sick with love and heartache for the Princess that his mother decided to give the King a visit, to ask for his daughter's hand in marriage to her son.

The servants at the palace sniggered at her before they guided her to the King. He was at first outraged, but then treated her gently and with tolerance, and asked what her mission was.

'I have come to ask for your daughter's hand in marriage to my son.'

The King remained silent while she described Bahram's love for the Princess to him. Then he said, 'I have listened to your wishes. In order for your son to take my daughter's hand in marriage, he needs to prove that he can provide for her. My request in this matter is that he pays a bride price of seven camels, each carrying two bags, one of silver and one of gold coins. On the wedding night the Princess must be wearing a crown made of seven large diamonds. In addition, seven Persian carpets, woven with pearl, silver and gold threads, must be spread under her feet for her to dance on, on her wedding night.'

Bahram was delighted by the news and left his sick bed to attend to the orders given by the King, of which his mother had carefully taken note.

The town was decorated amazingly to celebrate the wedding of the King's only daughter, which continued for seven days and seven nights.

And so Bahram became the King's son-in-law.

The Prince of Tooran, the neighbouring country to the land of Persia, was devastated by the news. He planned to get revenge on the shrewd tradesman who had traded sacks of gold, silver and pearls for the Princess of Persia. He sent his most reliable confidante, Jilah, to make some enquiries at the source.

It took her three months to reach the palace of Bahram and Princess Mehrdokht. Knocking on the door of the palace and pretending to be a tired old traveller who needed rest and fluid, she won the Princess's sympathy, and day by day she was seen to, fed and cared for, by the Princess herself. Both made a strong bond with the other and it was apparent that an empty space where Mehrdokht had been longing to find a mother figure had now been filled.

One day Jilah asked the Princess about her husband's wealth, how a simple tradesman could have become so wealthy, and whether she was aware of the secret to all his wealth.

'I have lived long enough to know that I have never seen or heard in any land that the son of a tradesman is wealthier than the King,' said Jilah.

The Princess did not have the answer to the question, but it made her think. She studied her husband's trading business and became more involved in the incomings and outgoings of the household. She suggested that she might help with the bookkeeping and accounts but still she couldn't make sense of the situation.

One day, quite exhausted with the dilemma, she asked Bahram, 'How is it that we are richer than my father, the King?'

Thrown by the unexpected question, Bahram replied, with half-smile, that it shouldn't really matter, but Mehrdokht felt puzzled and rather confused, and asserted that, as his life partner, she should know. Bahram felt nervous about telling her the secret that he had been keeping for years and ignored her request.

As the days passed, Mehrdokht became more and more distant from Bahram, and more attentive to Jilah. Bahram found these conditions hard to accept, and finally decided to tell his wife everything.

'I have broken my oath for the love that I have for you, but you must promise not to tell anybody, or else we will fall on hard times,' he added, before taking his wife in his arms.

Relieved by the news, Mehrdokht then told Jilah, to settle her mind about the dilemma too. Crafty Jilah sought an opportunity to find the ring, where she had been told it was kept. She immediately left the palace and Mehrdokht to take the ring to the Prince of Tooran, who had become very impatient.

As soon as Mahan, the Prince of Tooran, put the ring on his middle finger and rubbed it, he asked the genie for Princess Mehrdokht.

When Bahram returned from his business trip, he found the servants lamenting the Princess's absence. He realised that the ring was missing. Powerless, overwhelmed by the loss and on the verge of losing his sanity, he left the palace and walked around the city for days.

The dog, the cat and the snake, who had observed his pattern of behaviour, wandering like a ghost both night and day without ceasing, decided to help the hero who had once saved their lives with his own life investments.

The snake suggested that he should stay in the city, keeping an eye on Bahram, while the dog and the cat set off to the land of Tooran, where it was rumoured that the Princess had been taken to. They crossed deserts, climbed, hills and mountains, until they arrived in the city that was the capital of Tooran.

In the palace, no one really took any notice of them and they freely wandered about, trying to find the whereabouts of the ring. As the weeks passed, knowing that they were short of time and having had no success in finding the ring, the dog and the cat decided to approach Princess Mehrdokht and seek her advice in the matter.

Locating Princess Mehrdokht seemed easy, but finding her on her own, without any servants or guards surrounding her, proved to be impossible.

Finally one afternoon, Princess Mehrdokht, complaining of a headache, left the afternoon tea table and asked for privacy in her bedroom.

The dog and the cat sneaked into her bedroom and sat next to her bed, until the Princess started to stroke them, wondering at what good friends they were, despite being different species.

'We are friends who came together through sharing a similar history, having been saved by your husband Bahram,' one of them said to her.

The Princess sat up and, with a lump in her throat, asked, 'How do you know my husband?'

'He saved our lives with the money that he was supposed to have invested in business, and the snake, who is now nursing him while we came to look for you, gave his inheritance, the ring, to Bahram, as his and his family's gratitude for having saved his life,' explained the two animals briefly, sharing the story between them.

'I want to go home,' pleaded the Princess, miserably.

'You shall! We will make sure of that, but first we need to find the ring. We have looked everywhere, every little hole or hiding place possible,' they exclaimed.

'I know that Mahan stops talking and eating and has to brush his teeth right after dinner. I have always been puzzled by his peculiar routine, but it has made me wonder whether he keeps the ring in his mouth in the evening,' the Princess said.

The dog and the cat left to forge a plan to discover the truth about the ring's hiding place.

That very same night, the cat caught a mouse. The mouse, in terror for its life, promised the cat to be its confidante. The cat told the mouse to dip its tail in pepper, creep into the Prince's bedroom, climb up on to the bed and push its tail into Prince Mahan's nose.

When the mouse did this, the Prince gave such a violent sneeze that the ring flew out of his mouth, but the dog was in place to catch it high in the air.

The cat and the dog both set off, without catching their breath, to take it back to Bahram, whom they could hardly recognise, he had grown so weak.

Bahram put the ring on his middle finger with the help of his friends, and asked for his wife back.

He then treated his friends to a life of luxury. Once he had made sure that he and his family were safe and prosperous, he threw the Ring of Solomon deep into the Caspian Sea.

Bahram and Princess Mehrdokht and their children lived happily ever after.

SIX

The days had become longer and the evenings shorter. It was hard to sleep when the sun had not set, but the apartment was fully equipped with blinds and the rooms could be darkened to fool our senses and finally put us to sleep as late as 10pm most nights. We enjoyed the lighter and warmer days and spent a lot of time cycling, picking berries, eating ice creams and exploring the culture of the Swedish spring and summer.

While cycling back from school in the afternoons, we learned from observation that Swedish people spent a lot of time in their gardens during summer, planting, weeding and in general caring for nature, believing it to be a form of therapy.

The communal outdoor tennis courts became fully booked by eager players; the parks were busy with picnic baskets and children running around throwing frisbees; the lakes were packed with topless vitamin D-starved women as well as men and children, all bathing in the freezing cold water and calling it 'pleasant'. The swimming clubs, both outdoor and indoor, were full of children who wanted to enjoy the first breezes of summer. Campfires were also popular with young people, who would *grilla korv*, barbecue sausages.

At school preparation for the summer had already begun. The final school workload had come to its end, the school disco was being advertised and the celebrations for 6th June, the day of Swedish independence, were the talk of the school. The cake had been ordered, according to Ulla, the headteacher had been informed of the time to raise the flag, snacks were being prepared by the school kitchen, the games had been chosen, and in honour of the day the two senior classes of the year had to compete in a game of *brännboll*, Ulla announced in class a few days before the day.

My head spun for a minute at the news.

'You mean us?' I asked.

'You and Turkan will be in the same team, of course, against the other class,' Ulla explained calmly.

'*Brännboll*?' asked Turkan.

I shook my head.

'We hate *brännboll*,' we both said out loud in one voice.

'Come on, don't be like that, it'll be good fun. Your parents will be there to support you.'

My head spun once again. Ulla's confident comment, which was meant to be a comfort, had started our nightmare. It was not enough that we would have to play and compete in a sport that had been introduced to us only yesterday, as it seemed, but we would also have other children's parents watching, some in sympathy, calling out '*Vad synd!* (What a shame!)' if the ball was missed, while others would be cursing us for missing the ball.

'You are both taking this way to seriously,' Ulla said, interrupting my thoughts as if she could read them. 'These kinds of events and sports are supposed to be fun. It is not the winning that counts; it is the participation,' she tried to reassure us.

We both burst out laughing.

'Now, that's just rude,' Ulla said, and killed our laughter.

'Sorry,' we both said, but I continued, 'Have you been to our class? Have you met our classmates? What you say sounds perfect in theory, but the reality is that we are never picked for a team because we can't play *brännboll*. We are cursed by our team players and cheered by the other team for scoring *them* points. They want to win, and we are unwanted by our own team but truly desirable to the opposing team.'

'Listen,' Ulla said in a softer voice. 'This is a Swedish game which they have been playing from a very young age, and which you have only just been introduced to. You need to practise – practice makes perfect. Why don't you borrow bats and balls from Nisse and practise outdoors after school? You have a week until the match!'

We looked at each other, nodded, took her good advice, borrowed bats and balls, and met every afternoon under our balconies, where Kärringen had fallen, a few hundred metres from the naked lady, and practised.

We only had a week and every day we seemed to get worse at it. Perhaps we were distracted by imagining how terrible the game would be, or perhaps it was because we didn't have an instructor to teach us properly.

'You need to throw the ball higher!'

'Not that high, lower!'

'Don't hold the bat like you're playing cricket; hold it like you're playing baseball!'

'Hit it hard, not so low!' were comments that became famous in the neighbourhood for as long as we lived there.

'I admire your determination,' a lady said one day from her garden. She lived in a semi-detached house not far from where we were playing, and caught our attention.

'We don't know how to play and we've only got two days left to practise,' I said, smiling and feeling a bit embarrassed at having an audience when we were practising so badly.

'Well, I would have taught you if I weren't so busy packing,' she said, and sighed, seeming tired of her own commitments.

'Are you moving?' I asked.

She nodded, while continuing to pile the packed boxes in her back garden.

'We can help!' I suggested, secretly longing for a break from our practice.

She looked up and said, 'Only if you insist,' and smiled.

We helped move the boxes out while she packed non-stop, and then we helped her pack the kitchen stuff.

'Why are you packing on your own?' I asked curiously. 'I mean, where is your husband to help you?'

'I'm divorced,' she said.

'I'm so so sorry!' I said, feeling intrusive.

'It's OK. It's what I wanted.'

'Was he hitting you like Urban was hitting Kärringen?' I asked.

'No! We were just bored in the relationship.'

I didn't ask any further but caught Turkan's eye. She looked as puzzled as I felt.

'What about your mum?' I said.

'She lives in a home.'

'In her own home, you mean?' Turkan asked.

'No – in a nursing home.'

'Do you have brothers or sisters?' I asked.

'What about them?'

'Couldn't they help you?' we asked.

'It's not like that here. I have been to Greece so I understand where you are coming from, but here people manage to bear their own burdens and are happy to do so.'

'Sounds lonely,' we both said.

'Yes, to you who are used to having family around. We quite enjoy our own space. But you may call it loneliness,' she explained calmly.

We went on working until there was nothing more in the kitchen to pack, all the time feeling sorry for her.

Before saying goodbye, she handed us a ten-crown note and said, 'Well, why don't you go and buy some Varsil ice cream?'

'Of course, we'll be right back,' I said, taking the mission very seriously.

'Where are we going?' Turkan asked, while taking jumbo steps trying to catch up with me.

'Didn't you hear her? She asked for "Varsil" ice cream!' We would have to cycle to Vivo (our nearest supermarket) and find it quickly, then be back in no time for our practice. 'Actually, I think it will be a nice break and distraction from trying to hit a tennis ball with a baseball bat,' I said, shaking my head at my fate.

We quickly cycled to Vivo and looked in the freezer for individual ice creams but couldn't find any. We then moved to the dessert ice-cream section and looked thoroughly but couldn't find any Varsil ice cream. We went back to the individual ice cream freezer and looked at each pack one by one but found nothing.

'Now what?' Turkan asked, looking at me for a solution.

'Well, we'll just have to ask the shop assistant,' I said, and called for one.

The assistant went through all the boxes in both freezers and found no Varsil ice cream.

'I don't even recognise the name of this ice cream. Let me check our catalogue to see if we even stock it,' she said patiently. She looked through the list but found nothing.

'What do we do now?' Turkan asked me helplessly.

'We just have to cycle to ICA in Heidenstam Square,' I said, and sighed.

'But that's twenty minutes away,' Turkan pleaded.

The shop assistant, who heard us discussing our dilemma, kindly offered to call the ICA shop to save us some time. After a few minutes she came back, not looking very hopeful. She shook her head as soon as she met our desperate gaze.

'I'm sorry!' she said. 'You could always try the kiosk next door. They tend to stock unusual ice creams.'

We ran to the kiosk, looked at the ice-cream list a few times until the assistant asked, 'Can I help you?'

'We are looking for an ice cream which seems to be very rare and hard to find – Varsil ice cream,' I said.

'I see! Well, you won't find it here, either,' he said.

Absolutely desperate for some Varsil ice cream, we sat on a bench outside Vivo.

'What do we do now?' Turkan asked.

I thought for a few moments, while Turkan waited patiently. Then I suggested that we went back and told the lady that Varsil ice cream was out of stock. Looking back to that day, I am not sure why I suggested that; perhaps I felt too embarrassed to have failed at the mission given to us by a Swedish lady. Saying that it was out of stock made it the shop's responsibility, rather than our failure.

We cycled back and left our bicycles outside her door. The front door was open, but we rang the bell anyway. We heard a voice inviting us in.

'We are sorry, but Varsil ice cream was sold out,' I said sadly as soon as I saw her walking towards us.

'Excuse me?' she said, as if she could hardly believe her ears.

'We tried Vivo, and the kiosk outside Vivo, and the shop assistant even called the ICA shop in Heidenstam Square, but they are all out of stock. It seems to be a very popular ice cream.'

'What is?' she asked, looking confused.

'*Varsil glass* (ice cream)!' I answered slowly, thinking that she must be overtired after packing all day long on her own.

'Not "*Varsil*",' she said. '"*Varsin*"!' Then she laughed.

'Oh, I'm sorry – we heard you say "*Varsil*". That must have been the reason why we couldn't find it. We'll be right back,' I said, and turned to cycle back to Vivo.

'No no no!' she said, still laughing. '"*Varsin*" means "each" in Swedish. I wanted you to buy an ice cream each, for yourselves!'

'Oohh!' I said, but couldn't think, let alone speak.

'My name is Lisa, by the way,' she said, before we left her home for good.

SEVEN

The *brännboll* match was a disaster as expected but luckily our families were not there to witness our humiliation. We were the last ones to be picked, as expected. All eyes were on us (children as well as their parents) as we chose the lighter and thicker bats and held the balls very near the bat to hit it at least a metre, to give us time to reach the first stop. We waited for the next person to hit a home run so we could move on.

Some clapped, some cursed and some offered their condolences – 'What a shame!' – as a comfort.

We couldn't wait until the game was over and we could at last get on with our lives. Heads down, embarrassed but to an extent relieved, we were making our way back to school to seek comfort from Ulla when we saw Shahin lying on the playground, with Ali, a boy from Year 5, using him as a punch ball, hitting him on the face. I screamed as soon as I saw the scene.

'What are you doing? Let him go!'

But he continued as if he was deaf.

As I got closer I saw blood on Shahin's face, on Ali's hands and on Shahin's shirt. I could hear Shahin pleading, 'My dad sent me this shirt from Iran. He went to a lot of trouble sending it to me, now there is blood on it.'

I saw red and pulled Ali off my brother. He was an under-sized boy with a loud voice.

'If you ever touch my brother again, you will be beaten by a girl so badly that you won't be able to show your face around this school again,' I said. He saw in my eyes that I meant it.

'Do you understand me?' I asked, not sure how much Swedish he knew. He nodded.

I let go of him. I calmed my brother down. His nose had been bleeding so we needed to keep his head slightly up and calm him down until his nose stopped bleeding. Ulla, who had witnessed the scene from the window, came to help.

We took Shahin inside and called for the school nurse. He was mostly concerned about his shirt and tried to take it off to wash it. It was ripped, blood-stained and very dirty.

'We need to call your mum,' the nurse said.

'No! We don't!' I said. 'She has enough on her plate. She doesn't need to hear that her son was beaten up until he bled in a so-called safe country. Her only consolation in being so far away from home and her family is that we are safe from scenes such as these,' I said loudly.

Ulla approached me and put her hand on my shoulder. 'Perhaps I can speak to Shirin and Shahin's mum, on your behalf, Nurse Kerstin. Could you please see that Shahin receives the appropriate care?' Ulla suggested, calmly.

Turkan had gone to speak to Ali, who was Kurdish from Turkey, like her. She came back and explained that he wanted a piece of chewing gum from Shahin, and as Shahin was out of gum, Ali became very angry. The next thing he knew, he was at Shahin's chest, punching him. 'Ali is aware of his lack of control over his anger,' she said, shaking her head sympathetically.

I saw red once again – I was fuming. 'I'll give him chewing gum,' I said, and stood up. Turkan blocked my way.

Ulla said, 'Look, I suggest that you let it go—'

'You do, do you? My brother was beaten up, so his favourite shirt – his *only* favourite, because it had been sent by my father from Iran – was soaked with his blood. The only thing he cares about is the shirt that is ruined, and not his integrity, which was demolished – over a piece of *gum*? And you're suggesting that I should let it go?'

Ulla dropped her head, and Turkan stepped back while I collapsed on a nearby chair.

For the rest of the afternoon we became a speechless yet efficient team, trying to put the shirt back together again, washing it, sewing the buttons and pocket back on, mending it and ironing it.

When Shahin joined us from the nurse's office with a headache, he was happily surprised to see his shirt in one piece. We cycled back home together, and on the way he asked me to stop at the kiosk to buy some chewing gum.

'Listen,' I said, 'if you offer a bully something that he has asked you for, you will be in deep trouble. He will think that he has power over you and will misuse that power to get what he wants until the end of time.'

'What do I do?' he asked miserably.

'You don't give in. Ali won't bother you again. He has heard what I said and Turkan has spoken to him, and their families will talk about it too, so don't worry about him – but in the future, if you do not want to give anyone anything, don't! I am proud of you, Shahin, and I am not just saying that. I mean it. You did not hit back. You are twice as big as him, but you respected his size and were aware of his arrogance and pettiness.'

On that note we went home to Mum, had cuddles and her warm lovely stew made with herbs sent from Iran, and asked her to tell us again how she met Dad for the first time. She told us the story for the thousandth time and took us to the safe, familiar land of Iran before the revolution, war, uncertainty and utter chaos.

'I met him at the hospital cafeteria,' she started with a smile. The love story warmed our hearts. The sweet and sour tale with a happy ending made us believe that love overcomes all obstacles. It gave us hope that love would reunite us one day.

'Mum! Will we go back to Iran soon?' Shahin asked before going to bed.

My mum shook her head, as if she couldn't use words.

'Will we ever go back?' Shahin asked again.

'Never say never,' I joked, but no one laughed.

'Things are not getting any better in Iran. The war is worse than before—'

'Will Dad join us here then?' Shahin interrupted, as if he didn't want to hear any further.

'We have decided to allow a few more months, and if things don't get any better, he will join us.'

'What about the others, Maman Bozourg (maternal grandmother) or Meme (paternal grandmother)?' he asked.

'I think that it is too late to try and answer the questions that not even I have the answers to. Let's worry about it in the morning. Goodnight, darling,' she said, and kissed Shahin on the forehead. She obviously wanted to avoid the question.

EIGHT

Midsommarafton (Midsummer's Eve) is celebrated in June on the longest day of the year in Sweden. Raising and dancing around a *majstång* or *midsommarstång* (maypole) is an activity that attracts families and many others. Before the maypole is raised, foliage and flowers are collected and used to dress the entire pole. People dance around the pole to traditional music and sing songs such as '*Små grodorna*' associated with the holiday. Some wear traditional folk costumes or crowns made of sprigs of wildflowers. The year's early potatoes, soused herring and pickled herring, chives, sour cream, beer, schnapps, and the first strawberries of the season are on the menu. Drinking songs (*snapsvisor*) are also important at this feast, and many drink heavily.

We were excited by what we had learned about this day, and its programme, and couldn't wait to lift *majstången* and let the party begin. The sun was shining, which made a difference; it shone until it set near eleven o'clock at night. We cycled to our local neighbourhood park just in time to pick flowers for the pole. The blonde Swedish girls, sitting on the grass braiding daisies and wildflowers in crowns to decorate their heads while they danced around the pole, praising the sun and the light, looked like fairies in the golden sunshine.

Some wore their traditional Swedish folk clothes in bright colours of blue or red, with white or bright yellow aprons. We didn't really fit into the fairy tale but were just as excited about the ritual. We were invited to take part, which we happily accepted. We helped to decorate the *majpole*, helped raise it and for a moment felt proud to be involved in the process while we looked at the Swedish flag.

The musicians started playing and singing while dancing around the pole. We soon joined in, imitating the dance moves, the singing rhymes and hand gestures.

After the dances we were offered cream cake, decorated with fresh strawberries, *jordgubbs tårta*, and *jorgubbs saft*, strawberry squash. It tasted heavenly.

The afternoon was full of joy, laughter and fun. Turkan, Shahin and I made the most of the lovely sunny day and sat on the hill reviewing the afternoon, the rituals and the dance routine, and missing Ulla. It had only been a week since we had finished school for the summer holidays, but it felt like a month. She was the grandmother figure who completed the family frame.

We waited for the sunset, which seemed to take its time. We found the experience of our first longest day in this land near the North Pole quite astonishing. While we were waiting Shahin and I took Turkan down memory lane to Iran, and told her about the celebrations of Jaşne Tiregân, which is the ancient Iranian festival corresponding to the Swedish midsummer festivals.

This event is celebrated on the thirteenth day of the month of Tir, the fourth month of the Persian calendar, which equates to the 2nd or 3rd July in the Gregorian calendar. Iranians celebrate this occasion by dancing, singing and reciting poetry. During this celebration children and adults enjoy themselves by swimming in streams and splashing water on each other. The custom of tying rainbow-coloured bands on their wrists, which are worn for ten days and then thrown into a stream, is also a way for children to rejoice. Amongst Zoroastrians, it is a celebration of religious value as well as a joyous occasion.

We told her about the day at the Kushke Varjavand gardens in Karaj, and how we used to gather there for a picnic and looked forward to being splashed with water and splashing water on others. The day was filled with merriment and laughter, eating *aash* (thick noodle soup), dancing, music, and *faal* (*faal* is a question that you ask the universe about a wish close to your heart; you will receive the answer in the form of a poem), specified for the event of Tiregân. The celebrations would carry on late into the night.

'Tell her the story, Shirin,' Shahin said excitedly.

'What story?' Turkan asked.

The story goes that…

At the end of the war between Iran and Turan, the rulers of both countries decided to make peace and establish the boundary between their kingdoms.

It was decided that somebody would climb Mount Damavand, and from its summit shoot an arrow towards the east. Where the arrow landed would determine the new border. This was not an easy task to volunteer for.

On the bright morning of Tiregân, the best archer in the Persian army, Arash Kamangir, faced north, strained his bow and let the arrow fly as never before, the entire morning until noon, when it fell near the River Oxus. The river remained the boundary between Iran and Turan for centuries.

Arash Kamangir has remained one of the most popular of legendary Persian heroes. He is a symbol of sacrifice and bravery in Persian history. He will live in the memory of the Iranians forever, and is loved and celebrated at Tiregân for his goodwill.

On that note, wrapped in the warmth of tales on the longest day in the year, we three, who had made a pact to stay up until sunset and wake up again at sunrise to witness and experience the beauty of the magical *midsommarafton*, lost the battle, headed home, fell asleep and missed the few dark hours of the shortest night.

NINE

The month of July had provided us with enough sunshine to enjoy the summer holidays. We felt blessed and grateful. We had filled our days with bathing in the lake nearest to Uppsala, cycling, picking berries, eating ice cream, watching English movies rented from Vivo, playing ping pong and chess at the local youth club, while we missed school, well, mainly Ulla and her lessons.

That summer, at a chess tournament at the youth club, I came first and felt proud to receive the announcement, certificate and the honour. I was also asked to accompany the youth club to a tournament campsite in the Uppland region.

I asked Mum, and when the youth leader explained the trip to her and promised to call her on a daily basis, and also to keep a close eye on us all, she accepted.

The disappointment hit me when I realised that Turkan wasn't coming with me.

It was supposed to be for five days and was a camping trip, which meant that we were travelling by bus and would have to learn how to put up tents, light campfires, make dinner on an open fire and survive in the wild.

'Live like gypsies,' I said, while telling my mother about the arrangements.

'It'll be an experience, you'll learn from it and besides, you'll play your favourite game every day. Just remember to play it for fun – you don't have to win,' she said calmly.

I thought about the outdoor life, which was utterly unknown to me, and smiled to think that it would be a new experience, which I welcomed with open arms.

When the morning came, I said goodbye to my mum and Shahin, and went downstairs to find Turkan, but she wasn't home. I walked off with my backpack filled with clothes for all weathers (raincoat, swimming costume, warm jacket, sweatshirt, spare clothes, as well as a towel, pyjamas, torch, hairbrush and toothbrush) to the youth club.

Turkan was waiting for me outside the club and gave me a proper hug for good luck. She stood outside the bus and waved to me as it drove off, until I could no longer see her.

When I turned around, I saw about twenty Swedish boys and girls, speaking loudly and briskly in Swedish. I closed my eyes, attached the headphones to my Walkman, which I wore on my hip, and shut all the noise out.

We arrived at a camping site not far from the city of Uppsala. It was green, near a lake and had facilities such as communal toilets, with showers nearby.

With a lot of help from our youth leaders we put the tents up. Helena and I, who were sharing a tent, were among the last ones setting it up. Then we jumped into the lake and made the most of the noon sunshine. The water was ice-cold, but we enjoyed it thoroughly.

Later in the afternoon we helped build the campfire and barbecued plenty of hotdogs (*korv*), while singing along to the guitar someone was playing in the background. It was nice, different, but reminded me of our family get-togethers in Iran.

When I yawned, I knew that it was time to make my way back to my tent. I also wanted to wake up fresh for the next morning's chess match.

As I was creeping in my fleece pyjamas into the sleeping bag, I saw the light from a torch outside my tent.

I sat up.

'Are you awake?'

I recognised the voice. 'Is that you, Mats?' I asked.

'Yes, are you awake?'

'I wouldn't have replied to your question if I wasn't. What do you want?' I said irritably. Mats was a blond, very popular boy. He had blue eyes and was good-looking, and he knew it. He was good at chess but not brilliant, and he always watched me closely when I was playing and asked about my chess techniques. I guessed that he wanted to ask me about chess before tomorrow morning, so I zipped down the tent.

'Yes?'

'You were actually ready to go to bed?' he asked in surprise.

'I *was* in bed.' *If one can call a sleeping bag on a thin under-layer on the hard and cold ground a bed*, I thought.

'Do you want to join us in a midnight dip in the lake?' he asked, with a cheeky grin.

'A what? In where?' I asked, fixing my gaze on him, thinking that he must be joking.

'A dip! A dip in the lake that we were swimming in today,' he said with a smile, pointing to the lake.

'No, thanks! I need my sleep, and so do you if you are going to participate in the match, especially against me,' I said with a half-smile, and zipped up the tent.

'Wait… Shirin…wait!'

'What is it?' I asked, wriggling back into my sleeping bag, not bothering to zip the tent down again.

'*Vill du bli ihop med mig?*' he asked.

What the hell does that mean? I thought.

'So what do you say?' he said after a while, not realising that I was trying to figure out what he was asking me.

I didn't want to make the same mistake as the *Varsil glass*, so I zipped down the tent, looked him in the eyes and asked, 'What do you mean?'

'You know! That we can be girlfriend and boyfriend,' he said.

'And do what?' I asked.

'You know, we can hold hands, watch movies together, eat ice cream and go to the school disco together…' He was struggling to find an appropriate explanation to persuade me to accept his proposition.

'We are only twelve, Mats—'

'Sorry, I didn't realise – aren't you allowed?' he interrupted me.

'I'm not sure if I am – I haven't asked and don't intend to. I need to sleep and so do you. Please go and have fun or go to bed, and I'll see you in the morning.'

'Perhaps Helena would like to be my girlfriend,' he said arrogantly.

'Why don't you ask her?' I said unhelpfully.

The night was long, too cold, too noisy, too windy and the bed arrangements soon proved to be the most uncomfortable thing that I had ever agreed to. The insect bites, the noises from the excited children who were running about, chasing each other around the tents, made it impossible to sleep; and if that wasn't enough, Mats started to play his guitar outside our tent, singing love songs.

God save me, I thought. *Five days of this and I will die!*

I turned to my left and to my right, shut the world out and tried to concentrate on the game in the morning and feel positive about what the next day would bring.

I dreamt of the Caspian Sea; I was swimming, while Mum yelled not to go too far. I swam happily, waving back at Mum, trying to follow her advice. The water got cooler the farther I swam and I felt heavy in the water, as if the sea was swallowing me down. I noticed that I had my clothes on while swimming and had to swim back to the shore to take them off. I soon became tired and struggled as I swam. I felt wet and cold in my dream, and could hear splashes as I thrashed about in the sea.

I woke up in a pool of water, wet and freezing cold. I looked at my watch; it showed 4am. It was raining and must have been for the last hour. It had soaked through the tent. I didn't know what to do and didn't want to wake Helena. She seemed to be quite unaware of the situation and was fast asleep.

The clothes in my backpack were dripping wet, as it had soaked up all the rain from the wet ground. It was as though we were sleeping in a lake. I didn't know what to do.

I left the tent, which soon proved to be a terrible idea. It was raining heavily and there was no shelter. I sought refuge in the bathroom, took my clothes off and dried the items one by one under the hand dryer. It took a long time, but I was determined to go back to sleep in dry clothes. By now it was light outside and had probably been so for a long time. I felt like finding the youth leader's tent and asking her to take me home, but I waited until my clothes were dry. I put them back on, went back to our tent and read my half-soaked book in my soaked sleeping bag until 7am.

It was raining still. I saw my youth leader heading to the shower room and I caught her.

'Please take me home,' I pleaded.

'Good morning, Shirin!'

'Yes, a very good morning, but I need to go home,' I said anxiously.

'Why?' she asked, finally noticing my despair.

'I haven't slept since four o'clock in the morning. Our tent is flooded! My clothes are soaking wet, muddy and cold! I'm cold! The mosquito bites itch and I'm overtired!' I said, and burst into tears.

She held my shoulders, looked me in the eyes and said, 'What about the match?'

I just shook my head.

'Only if you're sure,' she said.

'I am,' I said.

Before I got on the bus, Mats said, '*Jag är ihop med Helena.*'

Knowing what it meant now, I said, 'Good for you!'

I crept into bed as soon as I got home and slept for the rest of the day. I woke up to my mum's famous omelette. Turkan joined us for the omelette and I told them all about the experience, and we all had a good laugh about it.

'Did Mats really ask you out?' Turkan asked, as we stood on the balcony looking at the sunset.

I nodded.

'And you said no!'

'Something to tell my grandchildren when they are my age,' I said.

'How silly you were, rejecting the offer, you mean!'

'Ha! No! How a blond, blue-eyed, popular Swedish boy asked me to "*Bli ihop med honom*" and I didn't even understand what he meant!'

We laughed until our eyes were filled with tears.

TEN

Mum excitedly laid out the plan for the following week, which had been organised by Auntie Sahar's church, where her husband was a preacher. I had not seen her so alive and excited about anything in all the time that we had been in Sweden. It made me happy too.

She told us that we would be travelling in a coach to the side of a lake in the south-west of Sweden. The camping site would provide accommodation, meals, evening entertainment and different activities and sports for all ages.

We became as excited about it as she was, although at the back of my mind the memories of my previous camping experience played a miserable tune. I decided to keep them to myself, as Mum and Shahin were so thrilled about the whole idea.

Going to the lake on the coach reminded me of being in Iran, when I used to travel to the seaside with my extended family. Now, throughout the journey, everyone passed the time singing, and even though we did not know the songs, we joined in and followed the rhythm.

At the campsite the rooms were simple and clean. They contained a single bed for Mum and bunk beds for Shahin and me, which kept us entertained while we fitted our pillows and duvet covers, before we went to explore the rest of the campsite.

The camp was set in a field, which was as green as it could be. There was plenty of space for sports such as badminton, volleyball and *brännboll*. The lake nearby was not only tempting for swimming; it also offered fishing and canoeing. The kitchen and dining room were open for breakfast, lunch, dinner and snacks in between meals. An entertainment area was prepared for shows, drama and activities in the evenings. If the weather was too bad for outdoor activities, there was an indoor sports hall to use.

The day started with breakfast, followed by lessons in Swedish history, with a break for tea, coffee and snacks at ten. Lunch was served at twelve, promptly. Activities such as fishing, swimming and sport kept us occupied in the afternoons, before a shower and dinner at six. The evenings were filled with songs, music, drama, laughter and fun.

The instructors seemed kind and firm, as did the Swedish-language teachers. The families were 'good Christian' families, and the sports and activities were led by trained instructors. Best of all, Mum was happier than I had seen her since our arrival in Sweden. She spent most of her time with Auntie Sahar, she sang like she used to in Iran and stayed up until late with her friend, talking about anything and everything.

As soon as we thought that it could not get any better than this we were taken on day trips to nearby islands. These excursions were amazing, as we explored Swedish history and culture, and enjoyed good food, Swedish cider and lots of sunshine.

On that trip we learned that you could get messy with clay, we learned that you could sing in a different language, even if you had not mastered it fully. Mum learned to ride a bicycle, we all learned more Swedish, but mostly we learned to enjoy a Swedish summer.

We had formed a family with a group of people who were kind and friendly, which would make it even harder to say goodbye. We had fished together, sang, danced, swam and played sports such as volleyball, badminton and basketball.

I missed Turkan, but I learned to communicate and socialise with the Swedish kids – a group of naïve, blue-eyed, kind-hearted, Christian children who had not experienced a war, a revolution, lack of freedom of speech, fear of torture and the risk of becoming a political prisoner or a child soldier; a group of innocent children who believed in Santa, the Tooth Fairy, Jesus and 'Kumbaya, my Lord'. Their innocence and their protected childhood were enviable. To tell the truth, it also felt safe to act and live in their world, pretending to be from the same world, a 'normal' world, where children are supposed to be children and believe in Santa, Jesus and the Tooth Fairy.

Until one sunny day, while I was sitting by the lake, learning to fish with Stina, she asked, 'Why are you here?'

'My mum's friend's husband is the pastor of this community and—'

'No, I mean why did you leave your country to come here?'

I didn't know what to say – where would I begin? What would I say without ruining her rose-tinted fantasy of the world?

'It's complicated,' I started. 'We didn't want to, but we had to.'

'I would never leave my homeland,' Stina said, shrugging her shoulders proudly.

'You would, if you had to,' I said, with a hint of defiance.

'Why are you wearing Western clothes?' she asked after a while.

'What do you mean?' I replied.

'People in Iran are covered in black from top to toe, why aren't you? Isn't that a bit hypocritical of you, not to obey the dress code that your religion dictates?'

'I am not a Muslim – and besides, if you, as a Christian, were to travel to Iran, you too would have to obey the law and dress accordingly. And anyway, not all Muslims in Iran are happy with the dress code or the rules of the Islamic law.'

'Why don't they say so? Why do they not protest? They seem happy on TV gathering for the Friday prayers in their black chadors.'

'Yes, why *don't* they protest? Stina, let's pray for a day when we Iranians will be able to voice our opinions, feelings and ideas, no matter how anti-regime they may be,' I said with a sigh, getting tired of her ignorance.

I closed my eyes, and while Stina was praying, I thought of life before the revolution, before the war; I thought of life before the chador, life before making music was declared a satanic act, life before a hundred lashes in punishment for drinking alcohol. Life before searches of your private property by teenagers with guns and no manners but licensed to kill. Life before children were trained as soldiers in the name of God, not only for the protection of their

71

homeland but to die so they could enter Paradise. I prayed for a democratic Iran where people would have freedom of speech, where their votes would count and their voices could be heard. I prayed for reunion with Maman Bozourg, Meme and all our loved ones in a peaceful and loving land.

Then, as if she had read my thoughts, Stina said, 'Amen,' and gave me a hug.

'I'm not only glad you came to Sweden, I'm glad you came to the camp too,' she said.

'Me too,' I said. 'I'll have to teach Turkan to fish when we get back,' I said, as we skipped along.

'Who is Turkan?'

'My best friend,' I said. 'You'll love her.'

At the end of two weeks we returned home with wide smiles, positive energy and a backpack full of skills that we had gained at the camp. It was the first time that we realised that it was more difficult to say goodbye than before. It reminded us of the previous goodbyes we had said, to our family and friends in Iran.

ELEVEN

My teeth had never been cleaner; I could smell, taste and feel the cleanliness with the tip of my tongue, stroking my teeth and sucking air between them.

'Do you think that he will be as strict as Dr Javani?' I asked my mum, while we sat outside the dentist's surgery, waiting to be called in.

'Are you nervous?' Mum asked.

I thought about Dr Javani's way of working before I answered. He had been strict, firm and a true perfectionist. He would not touch your teeth if he did not believe that they were clean enough. He had studied in Switzerland and was a true believer in the need for his practice in Iran.

'Shireeen, Amani!'

'It's me,' I said, and stood up.

Mum winked at me as a sign of good luck.

I stepped in, knowing the routine, but waited for the tall blond nurse to invite me to sit down. I waited for the dentist to introduce himself in English and ask for permission to examine my teeth. I opened my mouth while he had a good look around with his probe.

I felt nervous – I knew that my visit to the orthodontist was long overdue. My teeth were probably all crooked and wrongly aligned, and he was noticing how badly they had turned out, because I had been waiting such a long time to be allocated to the only orthodontist in the city of Uppsala.

Feeling slightly annoyed, I tried to make out a story from a poster above my head. One story led to another and kept me amused until Dr Johanson said, 'Was this work done in Iran?'

'Yes!' I replied nervously, thinking that he would most probably criticise the work. I continued, 'Well, you know, you have to remember that Iran is at war with Iraq, and there are limitations to—'

'Amazing, just amazing,' he interrupted me, and kept repeating the word until he summoned Mum to join us.

Hesitantly Mum came in, with a big question mark in her gaze. I looked back at her – I was struggling with the same confusion.

She stared at the dentist.

'The orthodontistry used on your teeth has been done in an excellent manner. It is so perfect that I cannot find any fault with it, however hard I look. The latest technique from Switzerland has been performed on you in a land that we consider a third-world country. I am absolutely and utterly amazed.'

'And as you pointed out, young lady,' he continued, 'the country is at war, with limited access to materials and facilities.'

Equally amazed, proud but slightly annoyed at being considered as coming from a third-world country, we left the building.

'Shall we have tea and cakes?' Mum asked, with a smile.

'Would love to,' I said happily.

We chose our cakes, both taking a slice of green 'Princess *tårta*', a sponge cake with layers of fresh cream and jam, with a topping of green marzipan, dusted with powdered sugar and decorated with a pink rose.

We poured the tea and each took a mouthful of cake. With closed eyes, I let it speak to my tastebuds, and welcomed the sensation with a satisfied smile.

'Do you like it here?' Mum suddenly asked me.

'It's a nice café!' I said. 'We could have gone to Café Linne, but—'

'No, I mean, do you like the country?' she tried again.

'Well… I am getting used to it, I guess,' I said. I looked at her sad face, anticipating what was coming next.

'I'm finding it hard,' she said, with tears welling up in her eyes.

'They usually say you should give the living arrangements in a new country at least two years… that's what Ulla told us,' I said.

She nodded with her head down, trying very obviously to hold back her tears.

I pushed her plate of cake closer to her. She picked up her fork and tried her hardest to cut a piece. It was not an easy sight to witness, her struggle, which represented her struggle in the new country.

'I tell you what,' I said at last, breaking the excruciating silence.

She raised her head, which looked as if it weighed a ton, and fixed her gaze on me, as though she was hoping for some miracle to be offered.

I sat up straight and, clearing my throat with a couple of coughs, said, 'If you still feel unhappy by Christmas, we can move back! We can go home, home to Maman Bozourg, to Meme—'

'The war is getting worse, more people are leaving and your father…' And then she burst into tears.

'What about Dad?' I said, suddenly feeling the seriousness of the issue.

It was agonising to watch her in pain, to see her struggle, to finally be faced with what she had been wanting to tell me, ever since we had arrived.

I wanted to tell a joke, sing a happy song, dance on the table to cheer her up. I had never wished for a magic wand more than that day, to make her happy and make her pain go away.

'Your dad has decided to join us in a few months, so it means that we are going to live here until the war is over.'

'That's not bad news! Honestly, Mum, you scared me! I thought you were going to say that he had been harmed, disabled or even killed. He can join us in the safety zone until the war is over and then we will all go back home,' I said with a smile. 'Look at it this way, he will be with us so we won't have to miss him or worry about him, and we'll all wait together until it's safe to go home,' I continued, with excitement in my voice, trying to convince her.

'What if the war continues for year and years?' she said. 'What if it takes a long time before it's safe to go home, and what if, in the meantime, we lose our family members or, God forbid, the war to the Iraqis?'

I tried my hardest to sound like an adult. 'Well… the way I see it, we just have to take it one step at a time,' I said. 'It will drive us mad to focus on the distant future, especially when we do not have the answers to the questions. Dad

joining us is great news! Shahin has missed him so much –
we all have! Also you will feel much better – he will share
all the responsibilities that you have been burdened with
since we got here.'

'When did you grow up to be so wise?' she said, with a
smile.

'I'm speaking with your voice,' I said, smiling back.

'You sound more like Maman Bozourg,' she said.

'I miss her!' I said, and tried to hide my tears.

'I miss her too, but I just realised that I have you,' she
said, and handed me a tissue.

TWELVE

It rained on the first day back at school and it seemed that the only people who were excited about being back, sitting on the school benches with wide smiles before the bell had even rung, were Shahin, Turkan and me. Even Ulla was distracted and disappointed by the rain.

'There should be a policy about "No rain on the first school day",' she said, wiping the rain drops from her skirt. Picking up on our enthusiasm, she smiled back at us, while she ran her fingers through her hair.

'How was your summer?' she asked, sighing and clearly giving up on her wet clothes.

We looked at each other, thinking that only one of us needed to tell her about our summer, for we had spent most of it together.

'We missed you, we missed school,' I said, feeling truly happy to be back.

Ulla smiled.

'I am sorry to interrupt,' we heard Ruth at the door. 'This is Jalil, who is giving us the privilege of starting in our class from today,' she continued.

Jalil seemed shy. He looked down and only seemed comfortable when he could hide his light brown eyes behind his dark curls.

'Are you from Iran?' Shahin asked.

'No – I am an *Araghi*,' Jalil managed to say after a while.

We looked at each other, seeing Saddam Hussein right in front of us.

I had never seen an Iraqi before. I felt sick to my stomach. In theory he was our enemy: he was the reason we had had to leave our homes, family and loved ones. He was the reason we were in a daily battle trying to settle into an alien part of the world, being constantly rejected and reminded of our backgrounds. He was the reason that my mum felt ill, sad and homesick. Inside myself I cried, and dropped my head.

The smile left my face, as it gradually dawned on me what a struggle it was going to be to share lessons with him. I wanted to leave, not just the school but the city, the country.

If we were back in Iran, at least we would be able to openly and proudly fight the likes of him, I thought. I could fight him to defend my country, my homeland, my name and my honour, and I would be backed up by my nation. Here I have to ignore him, share my school, my class and my teacher with him against my will, and there is nothing I can do about that, I thought.

It was all too much for me to digest. I was getting a headache and I could barely concentrate on the lesson, while ignoring and avoiding 'my enemy'. I felt relieved when the bell rang.

I was hastily packing up my books when Turkan interrupted me. 'Shall we take the bus home? Or would you like to go to the library first?' she said.

'We have to go to ABF to meet Mum. Apparently they have a party for the first day of school.' ABF was the Swedish school for adults. I sighed, thinking of my headache.

'Gulbahar told me about it too, but I didn't think that you would be interested. But if you're going, I'll join you,' Turkan said.

'I am not interested,' I whispered, although then it occurred to me that it might take my mind off things.

Shahin, Turkan and I got on the bus. I was feeling slightly lighter and my mood was picking up. The weather had turned and we were joking and laughing about our assumptions about the ABF party this afternoon, until…

'Hold the door,' I heard Jalil say.

I ignored him and did not even turn to face the doors at the back of the bus. Shahin put his foot between them, which prevented them from closing. The sensors opened the doors immediately, and I cringed, as Jalil stepped on.

'What did you do that for?' I asked Shahin, between clenched teeth.

'You're always telling me to be kind,' Shahin said innocently.

'Not to *him*…' I stopped myself from saying more.

I felt my sickness coming back; I had two sets of eyes, from my best friend and my own flesh and blood, questioning my behaviour and my thinking.

We'll get off the bus soon enough, I comforted myself. I could hear laughter but could not join in. I couldn't reason with my way of thinking or change it in any way. I felt too homesick and too bruised in my soul, and had finally found my scapegoat.

It felt like the longest twenty minutes of my life. I held my thumb against the stop buzzer and pressed it as the bus rolled towards our destination. I stood right in front of the doors and waited for them to open, as if the bus was filling up with lethal gas.

Out of the corner of my eye I could see Shahin and Turkan giggling, perhaps not about me, although that's what it felt like – but I couldn't have cared less. I just needed fresh air. As we stepped off, I let out a sigh of relief but caught my breath when I saw Jalil getting off the bus too. I stood at the station, perhaps to see which direction Jalil was going, so I could choose another one. My feet felt stuck to the ground, even though I could see Shahin and Turkan walking towards ABF, still giggling (this time, probably, about me).

I felt tired. This whole scenario was taking more energy from me than I had wished.

When I saw Jalil moving towards the entrance of ABF and holding the door open for Turkan and Shahin, I wanted to scream. *He is everywhere, like a contagious contamination*, I thought.

I had two choices: either go inside, have a good time and ignore him, or take the next bus home.

I decided to go inside and tell Mum that I was going home, so she wouldn't worry. I couldn't stand my own thoughts and the negative energy surrounding me. I just wanted to go home, crawl under my duvet and have Maman Bozourg finding me hiding there, so she could share her words of wisdom with me.

The hall filled with noises, food, music and laughter. I looked for my mother amongst the crowd.

I couldn't believe my eyes when I saw Jalil standing next to Mum and her... new friend. Mum was sitting with a woman whom I hadn't seen before, looking over her exercise book, helping her with her Swedish!

'Since when have you become the teacher's assistant?' I asked, laughing at my bad joke while ignoring Jalil.

Mum looked up with delight and, with a big smile on her face, proudly introduced her friend to me.

'This is Gulshan,' she said.

I shook Gulshan's hand, who stood up and introduced her son.

'This is my son, Jalil,' she said.

I looked at Mum, thinking that she must know where Gulshan was from – yet she had unconditionally accepted her friendship and was helping her, passing on what she might know more about than her. I felt confused and asked her to accompany me to the food table.

She followed me to the table, to help me with the food. Shahin and Turkan were already eating with Gulbahar at her table.

'What's Gulshan's story, then?' I asked.

The look she gave me spoke a thousand words, none of approval of my comment or attitude, which she wisely chose to ignore.

'She is here with her son from Iraq. They only arrived two months ago. Gulshan, like me, misses her family in Iraq and is experiencing the tough life that we had when we first arrived, with all the same uncertainties and confusions. The cultural clash is devastating to us all.'

With no empathy at all, I said, 'They shouldn't have started the war, then! Such a nerve! Starting the war and then fleeing here to keep safe – that's Iraqis for you!'

Mum turned red, from embarrassment or anger, to this day I don't know which, but then she collected herself and explained, 'Gulshan and her family, like other Iraqi civilian families, did not start the war. Saddam Hussein did. They are as much victims of a war as we are! Victims of war, or survivors of the war, is a not a label to be owned exclusively by the Iranians. I will not tolerate such thinking and behaviour from my children with regards to Iraqis or any other nation. Before any religion, race or colour we are humans. They are suffering as much as we are, with heartache, missing their loved ones and struggling to learn the new way of life here. Your way of thinking will only harm you, lead you to lose out on friends and exclude you from the pleasure of being around people with quality.'

Then, in disappointment, she said, before walking off, 'I thought that I had been successful in bringing you up to love others, rather than judging them by the country that they come from.'

I felt so embarrassed. I walked towards Jalil. He was standing with our mothers, who seemed engaged in their homework. I gave him half a smile and said, 'I have a cousin your age, in Iran. His name is Ashkan.'

'You must miss him,' he said sympathetically.

Trying to hide my tears, I nodded.

THIRTEEN

In the six months that we had lived in Uppsala, we had hardly had any issues with our flat, as it was fairly newly equipped, until one morning, when my mum announced that the oven had given up on us. We tried all the switches, tested the fuses and twiddled the knobs on the electric oven, but the thing seemed completely dead.

At last we decided to call the local janitor to make an appointment for a visit. It was fairly straightforward, and he said that he would come around sometime between five and six in the afternoon. As the Swedes stick religiously to the times of their appointments, Mum made us promise to be home before five, so that we could have a family dinner before the janitor came. We promised.

At school we had a *Friluftsdag* – a field day – in which we all gathered in the woods and were supposed to locate various stations at destinations chosen by our PE teacher. At each one you had to punch a hole in a card with a device provided, to indicate that you had found the station with the help of a compass.

Nisse, our PE teacher, was the tallest man I had ever seen. He had a slightly bulbous forehead and always wore glasses. He seemed very proficient in all the theories of the sports that he introduced to us but never came up to our expectations when we witnessed him in action. I felt that I was being preached at about how to hold the bat, how to hold the racket or how to climb up the wall, while he never seemed to be able to demonstrate what he was preaching about in action himself.

Friluftsdag – a day out in the open air full of surprises, new experiences and beauty, which turned into a wet, cold, dark and dull October day, in which Turkan and I struggled to keep track of the stations and time, while we tried to learn how to read the compass. It was hard to ignore the rain, the mud and the chill in the air, in order to enjoy the Swedish countryside.

Realising that we were lost, Turkan and I were discussing the options and techniques for surviving the night outside in the cold and the dark, and going through the wild animals in the Swedish woods that we had learned about earlier in the health and safety induction, and fantasising in horror and amusement about being eaten by them, when we saw Nisse's head poking through the bushes.

'What are you girls up to now?'

'We got lost, we couldn't find our way back!' I said, with relief at seeing him.

'Everyone is waiting – we need to head back to school,' Nisse said, with some annoyance.

I looked at our station cards. We had only punched four stations out of ten. We handed them to Nisse with a touch of embarrassment but didn't say anything else as we just wanted to go home.

We didn't say much on the bus back home; we didn't even apologise for being late or having kept everyone waiting; we just sat in silence, reflecting on our lack of knowledge of nature exploration, compass-reading and *Friluftsdag* in general.

I finally broke the silence, as we cycled home together.

'Would you like to come upstairs to dinner?' I asked Turkan. She nodded.

'Where have you been?' Mum greeted us. She looked confused. 'I told you to be back by five! Where were you?'

I looked at her with surprise. I wasn't sure what she was talking about, until I saw the dinner table.

'The janitor,' I just managed to say, before the bell rang.

The kitchen table was all set for dinner, covered with the fruits of Mum's devoted labour in the kitchen. There was no time to eat it before opening the door, or even to clear the colourful table. I looked at Mum for an answer.

She had no choice. 'Open the door, will you?' she said.

I opened the door with a sigh. The janitor greeted us and asked us about the problem. I only offered half of my attention, as the other half was focused on my rumbling tummy, my hunger and the food on the table. Mum's cooking was always awesome, but it smelled and looked extra delicious this evening.

'Sorry to have disturbed your dinner,' the young janitor said considerately.

'Would you like to join us?' Mum offered. Standing behind the janitor, so he couldn't see me, I shook my head as a sign of disapproval.

The janitor turned around and looked at the table. 'Are you sure?' he asked. Mum nodded.

I was fed up, after a day full of unpleasant surprises and experiences. All I wanted to do was to take a shower, wash all the mud, smell and embarrassment off my body, have Mum's homemade meal, and then crawl under the sheets, but oh no, instead I would have to sit up at the dinner table, smile, be polite and make conversation with a stranger whom we'd met five minutes ago.

Mum went into the living room to call for Shahin and I followed. 'What did you do that for?' I hissed.

'What do you mean?' she asked.

'Inviting him to stay for dinner.'

'It's only polite,' she said firmly. 'We cannot eat while he's working.'

It made sense, and she sounded truly kind, but I still wanted to enjoy my dinner in peace.

The janitor pulled out a chair and sat down, getting his tastebuds ready for a new experience, while Mum set down a plate for him. Shahin, Turkan and I sat down with a sigh, accepting our defeat. Mum smiled as she sat down, realising that she would have to work extra hard at being friendly and polite, to cover the unpleasant atmosphere we had created with our objection.

We all ate in silence, until the janitor said, 'This is absolutely delicious! What's in it?' He sounded puzzled.

We all looked at each other, looked at the food and looked at each other again. I knew the names of the ingredients in Swedish, but trying to explain the cooking method and the actual recipe, translating in my head from Farsi into Swedish on the spot, proved to be more difficult than I thought it would be.

After a long silence, a cloud of confusion, a hint of desperation and a flurry of apologetic expressions from us, he interrupted. 'If you can tell me how it was made, perhaps

I can make it for my girlfriend.' Then he paused, and after a while said, 'I'm intending to propose to her next week.'

We were lost for words. I silently prayed for a miracle to rescue me from the kitchen. We felt pretty terrible for not being able to explain in words a simple recipe, and to add to the dilemma was his idea of using the dish as part of his proposal. It was all a bit overwhelming.

Instead, we somehow made a mutual and mute decision to continue eating, pretending not to have heard or to have understood him properly, silently hoping that he would move on to another topic and talk himself out of our misery.

He told us about his job, his girlfriend, his cooking skills and his speculation about the recipe of what he had just eaten. After he finished fixing the oven, he packed his toolbox and, with a homemade cookie in his hand and a face full of satisfaction, he left our flat.

After Turkan had left and Shahin had fallen asleep, I crawled into Mum's bed and curled up under her duvet. I found her silently crying.

'Cooking is my joy. It's a skill that I am proud of and I cannot even name the ingredients or the cooking method in the language of the country that we are living in.'

'Is this why you are crying?' I asked with relief.

'I feel like an invalid! I felt as if I were handicapped tonight! Not being able to describe the simplest recipe, that would take me minutes to do in my own language,' she sobbed.

'Well, did we need the language for it, though? He enjoyed the dinner so much that he left with a smile and even suggested that he would make it as a proposal dinner,' I said, laughing cheekily. 'Bless him, imagine making *lubia polo* for your wedding proposal dinner!' I went on. 'It would be equivalent to spaghetti Bolognese. It was lucky you didn't know how to say it in Swedish. You probably saved him from a lot of embarrassment.'

'Do you think so?' she asked, with slight relief at seeing the light at the end of the tunnel.

'Yes, I think so,' I said, and nodded. 'Who would say yes, over *lubia polo*?' We laughed so hard that we had to bury our heads under the duvet so as not to wake Shahin.

'You are the best cook, Mum!' I said, when we had calmed down. 'I will always remember this evening and tell it to my children and grandchildren, and have a good laugh about it,' I promised her. 'This reminds me of a story that Ulla told us in school,' I said.

'Is it a Swedish story?'

'I'm not sure of its origin, but it's a very sweet one...'

One cold evening, rainy and dark, an old woman was preparing to put her feet up and have a carrot for supper, when there was a knock on her door. A beggar stood outside the door of her cottage, asking for shelter.

'If you want food, my cupboard is as bare as a baby's bottom,' the old woman grumbled.

The beggar, who was cold and hungry, took a nail out of his pocket and said, 'This is a magic nail! I can make the most magnificent soup with this nail.'

Intrigued, the old woman led him into her kitchen.

The beggar filled a saucepan with water and put it on the stove.

'Nail, we trust that all your rust will make a tasty soup for us,' he said, then sat down and waited.

The old woman asked if the soup needed seasoning. 'Good idea,' said the beggar.

The boiling water was seasoned, but the woman worried about the soup and asked if an onion would add to the flavour. She came back from the larder holding a parsnip, a carrot and a potato, as well as an onion. They peeled and chopped the vegetables and put them into the pot.

The aroma filling the room made them both hungrier, until the beggar said, 'You know, some tender, lean meat would make an extremely good soup, an amazingly good soup.'

The old woman disappeared into the larder again and came back with a huge piece of steak, which she cut up and put it into the pot.

As the anticipation built up, the beggar asked her to set the table. The old lady brought out her best tablecloth, her china soup bowls, shiny silver spoons and candlesticks, with candles in them.

Again the beggar took a chance and said, 'It's a shame you don't have any food in the house, no freshly baked bread and wine…'

The old woman didn't let him finish his sentence. She hurried into her cellar and came back with a good old wine, two of her best glasses and a loaf of freshly baked bread from the morning.

'The soup is now ready,' said the beggar, and gently removed the nail and put it in his pocket.

They sat at the table and had a feast. After they had finished, the old woman declared that it was the best soup that she had ever tasted. As a gesture of gratitude, she offered him cheese, apple pie and chocolates, which were easily washed down with another bottle of wine.

They told each other stories and jokes until the candles burned themselves out.

FOURTEEN

It had been a long day at school. We had been given an assignment to write an essay about 'The Life of an Immigrant'. Moments like that, they don't only bring to your attention how much you miss your dad, and what seems to be your non-existent relationship with him; they also portray how much you lack when you start to write. How restricted you are left feeling, with your limited vocabulary in the language that you are trying so hard to adopt, psychologically, emotionally and with all your senses and power. Not being able to put my feelings into words and form sentences, describe, clarify and demonstrate my meaning seemed to be my new-found disability.

However, my teacher was happy with my progress and seemed totally ignorant of my annoyance with myself and my struggle. Mum relied on my language skills when it came to letters and forms that needed to be read, filled in and sent back. Turkan was proud of my progress and very encouraging. But I felt defeated and isolated in my loss of fluency.

While I was walking towards the school dining hall with my head down, I bumped into Glay. She pushed me so hard, she woke me from my miserable reverie. Like Turkan, Glay was from Turkey, but she wasn't a friend of mine.

'What are you doing?' I asked.

'You pushed me first!' she cried.

'It was an accident,' I said.

'So was mine,' she said, laughing so hard that her gang could hear her.

I saw red. I wanted to hit her, to push her again, and I could tell by the look on her face and her body language that she wanted me to do so. She pushed her face into mine, puffed her chest out and, screwing up her eyes, said, 'I dare you!'

I clenched my fist and gritted my teeth, already seeing my mum in the headteacher's room, discussing my behaviour and school detention, when Turkan's face appeared in front of me, as she hissed, 'It's not worth it!'

I knew that Glay and her gang would say that I was scared if I walked away now; in my mind I could hear them, imitating me with chicken noises. But then Turkan turned to Glay and said, 'How is your dad? He is coming to see us tomorrow, you know.'

Glay replied, and they carried on in Turkish. From what I gathered it seemed to be a friendly conversation, which calmed Glay, and they all walked away from the scene, leaving me with my teeth clenched and my brow creased with tension.

A couple of hours passed before we were allowed home. I wanted to avoid Turkan, which was not easy. She caught up with me near my bicycle and asked if we could cycle home together. I made an excuse, saying that I had to go to the shops to buy groceries. She offered to accompany me.

We made our way to the supermarket, where I really didn't want to go and had no reason to be. I stomped around angrily, wondering if this day could get any worse.

'You didn't need to do any shopping, did you?' Turkan asked.

Feeling embarrassed about the excuse that I had invented after she had actually saved me from my wicked self against Glay, I said, 'Here it is! It was here all along. I just couldn't find it.' I picked up a leek.

'A *leek*?' Turkan asked, looking confused. 'I have never seen your mum cooking anything with a *leek*,' she continued.

'You don't know my mum's cooking, my mum or even me! You don't know us at all! So don't pretend that you do. Because if you did, you would have known that I don't need anyone to save me from an evil creature like Glay.'

'So this is what's bothering you,' Turkan said with a sigh and a little smile. 'Look,' she went on, probably seeing the fumes coming out of my nose, 'it was more for her sake than yours,' she continued.

I didn't know how to take this, whether to be offended or to feel relieved.

'I'll show you! ...After you've bought your leek, of course,' she said, with a hint of sarcasm.

I paid for the leek and put it my backpack. I followed Turkan, cycling in an unfamiliar direction, with no questions asked.

Cycling in the cold and the dark towards the unknown linked well with my current situation in life, so we cycled in silence.

'We can park here,' Turkan said, getting off her bike. We were outside a block of flats.

I parked my bike next to hers. 'Now what?' I asked, annoyed.

'We wait,' Turkan replied calmly, and sat on the bench outside the flats.

So we did. We sat in the cold autumn evening, waiting in silence, until I stood up in protest.

'I don't know what you're trying to do or to prove, but I'm cold, hungry and have had enough of Glay for one day. I'm leaving!' I said.

Turkan looked at her watch and said, 'It usually is about this time... hmmm, I wonder if—' She was interrupted by a shriek.

We took shelter at the front door. It sounded like a cat being dropped in a tub of water.

'What is happening?' I asked, genuinely afraid of the response.

Before Turkan could answer, we heard bangs and crashes, followed by cries and screams.

It continued for longer than I prayed it would. After a while the sound of the beating changed, as though the victim were exhausted. Suddenly we heard quick footsteps down the stairs. I panicked and grabbed Turkan's arm; I tried to drag her into the bushes to hide, but she got stuck halfway, just as Glay came out, who caught sight of us in action.

She was bloody, black and blue. It was hard to see where she was bleeding from. Her nose looked crooked, her right cheek was cut open, her lips were swollen and her left eye was half closed.

'What are you looking at?' she asked. She was looking at us out of her right eye, trying to keep cool but sounding bitter and utterly vulnerable.

Half stuck in the bushes, I struggled out, straightened my clothes, wiped the dust off and said, 'Would you like my mum to have a look at your bruises and cuts?'

'Her mum is a nurse,' Turkan added quickly.

'What a wuss,' Glay said, and lit a cigarette.

I sighed. I felt angry for her, realising how she had adapted to the abuse, the beatings and the violence, pretending not to care.

Suddenly we heard a man shouting in the flat above where all the beatings had been happening. He kicked the balcony, yelled and muttered something.

Glay ran back upstairs and I started shivering, silently cursing Turkan for introducing me to this element of immigrant life in Sweden.

The yelling and kicking did not stop, but Glay managed to find her way back down the stairs again, with a bottle of gin in her hand. She relit the unfinished cigarette in her mouth.

'What is he saying?' I whispered to Turkan.

'Why is he here? Why was he born in a country where there is no freedom, so that he had to come over here to clean toilets, when in his own country he is an educated gentleman? What kind of a life is he leading? Why did he have to leave his sick mother and ill brother behind? What kind of a son and brother does he call himself? What is the meaning of this miserable life? And it goes on and on,' replied Glay to my question, without bothering to lower her voice.

'What happens now?' I asked those who knew the routine, to find out if we had all the unpleasant surprises out the way for the evening.

'This is the best part of the evening – this is when the party starts!' Glay said, handing me the cigarette.

I looked at it but then said, 'Smoking kills, you know.'

'Such a cliché,' she said, and took another drag on her cigarette. 'Have you ever known anyone to die from smoking?' She passed me the bottle.

I sniffed the bottle. It smelled strong, too strong for me even to try.

'No, thank you!' I said, and pushed the bottle back at her, feeling vaguely apologetic for coming across as a goody-goody.

'I'll have some,' Turkan said, trying to divert the focus of attention to herself, obviously wanting to avoid more conflicts for one day.

I watched while my best friend sacrificed herself with a slurp of gin, shaking with disgust. Glay poured half of the bottle down her throat in one go, without even blinking.

The wailing and the yelling from upstairs had stopped, but outside Glay's drinking and smoking were getting worse. I felt like vomiting and I did so, right there and then. It was too much for me to take for one day.

'A total wuss, I told you, the moment I saw her,' Glay said to Turkan, before muttering something in Kurdish and disappearing into the backyard.

We cycled home in silence, full of sadness. Deep down, I wished that I had hit Glay that morning, without a care in the world for her life or any need for awareness of it.

I cried at home under the duvet in my bed before seeking comfort in Mum's arms. I thought about my own dad, and whether he would turn out like Glay's father, full of losses, guilt and grief, hopelessly drowning in disappointment.

Before falling asleep, I thought of my essay and knew exactly what to write.

FIFTEEN

Turkan was running towards me. 'Shirin! You will not believe this!' she was shouting. After pausing to catch her breath, she went on, 'Ulla is going to read your essay in front of the whole Year 8 class in the senior school. They are talking about awards and things.'

I stood there, silent for a long time until she said, 'Did you hear me?'

'I think so!' I replied, sensing I was being praised but not understanding why.

'I am serious, Shirin,' she said as if she were reading my thoughts.

Feeling confused, I made my way to the classroom, with a very proud Turkan by my side. She was confident in my proficiency in writing, and in my passion for it.

Ulla was waiting for me at the classroom door, with a twinkle in her eye. She explained, with a wide smile on her face and pride in her voice, that my essay had been the talk of the school and that she had shown it to the headteacher and other teachers in the junior school, as well as the literature teachers in the senior school, who had read it and found it fascinating. She asked for permission to read it to the Year 8 students in the senior school, as they had all been working on the same subject.

I stood there, no doubt with my mouth half open, wondering whether I was hearing it right, whether I was understanding it correctly, whether I was dreaming.

'But my Swedish is not so… good,' I blurted out.

'Apparently it is as good as the Year 8 students,' she said with a smile.

I listened while Ulla made plans to see us after lunch, to take us to the lesson where she would read out the essay, but all I could think about was that I couldn't really remember what I had written. I went blank and mute and followed the others in to lunch and then to the Year 8 classroom, where two tall, blue-eyed, blond Swedish students were sitting, throwing paper aeroplanes, whistling and making funny faces, until Ulla was introduced. She then introduced me to the class. I looked around, facing their cold envy and their incomprehension, and I immediately sat down, wanting to apologise to the older audience for having been better than they were at writing on a subject that they had been working on.

The Immigrant

Oskar was feeling tremendous guilt, despite having been warned about it by his mother when she said goodbye.

The year was 1872 and Oskar was seventeen. He was fleeing the poverty in Sweden in the hope of making a better living in the land of opportunities. The letters from his uncle in Chicago were pretty convincing about the way of life in America.

Oskar was only nine years old when he lost his father. He remembered the night very vividly.

His father, Lars, was working at the Master's stable when the manor was set on fire. The fire spread wildly in the wind, with a life of its own, seeming determined to kill and destroy everything. In the screams and shouts and tally of the survivors, it came to everyone's attention that the Master was still in the manor.

In the blink of an eye Oskar's father ran inside, with no second thought. He never returned but died as a martyr, to save the Master's life.

The Master, who preached hereafter about how he owed his life to Lars, had many opportunities to show his appreciation, such as when Anna, Oskar's youngest sister, fell ill with a high fever and needed medical treatment in the city. She passed away soon after. Then there was the time when Oskar and his mother wanted to hold a decent funeral for his middle sister, who had fallen in the frozen lake and been found dead by the Pastor.

The Master had one last opportunity to support the remaining members of the family when Oskar asked him to lend him the money for his mother's fare to America. Oskar had only saved enough for one ticket. Instead the Master offered his mother a job as a washerwoman.

Before he left, Oskar's mother gave him a brooch that had belonged to his great-grandmother. She told him to sell it only if he became desperate for money. Oskar checked the value of the brooch to see if it could pay for another ticket, but it wasn't enough. He then asked the agent to reduce the price of the ticket, but he was refused. He had no option but to leave his mother behind.

'You'll come back for me, I know you will. You have to leave to make us a home across the Atlantic, find your way, work hard, make a living, save your money and then come back for me. You are doing this for us, Oskar. I'll wait for you,' his mother reassured him.

When 'Land in Sight' was announced, Oskar realised that something he thought had died was still alive inside him: hope, hope for a new beginning, hope for a better life, hope to make a better life for his mother, and hope to be happy again.

'Here we come, America!' yelled the children who had been victims of the longest boat journey, filled with cries, boredom and seasickness, waving as if the Americans were waiting at the harbour to welcome the Swedish immigrants.

Ulla had tears in her eyes and a lump in her throat. Turkan was also wiping her tears away. Listening to my own words made me feel proud, not really knowing where the words had come from. I felt numb. I didn't dare look at anyone else in the class and left the room with my head down.

Outside the classroom Ulla asked if she could send my story to the school council for a review and a possible award. I nodded. 'Was it really that good?' I asked doubtfully.

She put her hand on my shoulder, looked into my eyes and said, 'It was better than good!'

Turkan and I sat on a bench inside the school looking at the school lockers, wondering what it would be like when we started senior school next year. We day-dreamed about senior life until the bell rang and the hall filled up with older students. They all looked so cool, confident and focused; even the way they unlocked their lockers was cool, while they chatted over them, picked out their jackets and put their folders covered with Wham!, Madonna and

Michael Jackson photos under their arms, before they left, laughing together. It all seemed magical.

'I can't wait,' I said, looking at Turkan.

She nodded in agreement.

We left eventually, feeling happy about the insight into our future student life in Uppsala that we had earned.

Outside in the cold, Turkan remembered that she had left her cardigan inside and had to go back for it. She told me to start cycling home, saying that she would catch up with me, but I said that I would rather wait for her on a bench.

'Hey, you!' I heard someone yell amongst the students who were hanging around outside.

She came towards me so I that could see more of her. Actually, it was hard for her to go unnoticed. She was the biggest Swedish girl that I had ever seen. She was accompanied by a group of her own size and shape. It was hard to tell whether they were girls or boys. They all looked the same, as if they were in the army.

'Yes?' I asked.

Everyone on the senior school playground stood silent and still.

'Who do you think you are, coming to my country, trying to be smarter than me?' Big Girl asked.

'Who do I think I am? I know who I am! I'm Shirin. I thought that Ulla had introduced me to you all in your classroom,' I said.

There were laughs, whispers and giggles at my comment, which infuriated Big Girl even more.

'Are you making fun of me?' she asked, with an added harshness to her voice.

'You are doing that perfectly well on your own, you don't need my help for it,' I said calmly.

Big Girl came towards me.

I stood up.

Her gang followed behind her.

I could see that she was twice my size and I immediately regretted standing up, but I tried to keep my knees from shaking and locked eyes with hers.

'Hope you've written your will,' she said, pushing her face into mine.

I said nothing. Suddenly, I felt the warmth from another student standing on my right and soon after another one on my left, both whispering, '*Ma Irani hastim* (We are Iranians).' I smiled, still gazing into Big Girl's icy, bloodshot eyes.

Soon there was a line of Iranian senior students standing on either side of me, forming support and protection. I saw Turkan releasing herself from her Kurdish friends, who had tried to stop her from getting involved, coming to stand in front of me like a shield, saying to Big Girl, 'She is my sister. You hurt her, you hurt me!'

Glay joined us, shaking her head and mumbling to herself, probably cursing Turkan in Kurdish for getting involved, and gradually her gang of Kurdish girls from the senior school followed her.

We stood there, all from different backgrounds, religions, races and genders, and felt proud of our stand. You could smell the power of our unity in the air.

Big Girl spat on the ground. 'I'll give it to you, when you least expect it,' she said, before she turned to leave.

'Isn't that what cowards do?' I said, before I turned to my new-found friends and introduced myself properly. I felt protected and relieved to have made a group of friends from the senior school before I joined it, and all thanks to Big Girl – who turned out to be Finnish and did not own the country after all.

SIXTEEN

As Christmas slowly approached, the cold and dark winter days were filled with sparkle and magic. We were fascinated by the Swedish way of welcoming the birth of Jesus, beginning with Advent. Every Friday, starting four weeks prior to Christmas, one of four candles would be lit, while *pepparkakor* (ginger biscuits) and *Luccekatter* (saffron pastries) would be served, and the angelic voices of the choir singing carols filled the hall at assembly.

Walking home, I would watch through windows as Christmas trees were put up and decorated by families, and Christmas muffins were baked and Christmas decorations made, while mulled wine with almonds and raisins was drunk and children wrote their wish lists.

It was all so foreign, yet extraordinarily magical to us. Homesickness had never felt better.

It was on the day of the Feast of St Lucy, 13th December, when the tallest, blondest, blue-eyed girl in school would dress up as the Italian Lucia and walk through the dark early morning with candles in her hair, singing like an angel bringing light and salvation, that I met Claudia.

She was sitting in the front row, and kept hissing at me and Turkan to keep quiet. Her behaviour eventually became so annoying that I told her to mind her own business. She said that I was being rude, so I told her to change her seat if we were annoying her. We kept arguing until we were shushed by the music teacher, but then we all burst out laughing, when the Lucia of the year, who had assumed that the music teacher was referring to her, kept quiet, looking at us all, waiting to be given the signal to continue by the music teacher.

'Why couldn't you keep quiet?' Claudia asked me after the ceremony.

'Perhaps I didn't find it as interesting as you,' I said.

'What is not interesting about it? All that beauty, so magical, angelic and powerful,' she said.

'Is that what you saw? What I saw was a chosen blonde who was pretending to be a dark Italian, accompanied by a long blond-haired blue-eyed Jesus chosen for the nativity show, acting as a dark Galilean Jew,' I said, and sealed the argument.

'Oh dear, the things that you notice and get hung up about!' Claudia said.

Turkan shook her head in sympathy.

'Perhaps I don't have the need to believe in magic as much as you do,' I countered.

'If you had been hunted from the age of six by government security officers, hiding, running for your life and living underground with your younger siblings, only because your mother was fighting for her rights and for freedom of speech, you would've believed in magic and prayed every night to be saved by it,' she said, attacking back.

Looking into her big brown eyes my reason was swallowed up in her grief, to the extent that I joined her prayer for the magic to return.

'From the age of six until our arrival here, I always slept with my shoes on, in case we needed to flee during the night. I kept my toothbrush in my right pocket and one set of clean underwear in my left, fleeing during the night from house to house and sleeping during the day,' Claudia continued.

'Why didn't you leave the country?' Turkan suddenly asked, while I still felt stuck in Claudia's grief.

'My mother was a strong believer in women's rights. She was a very brave lady who fought on behalf of all Chilean women,' Claudia explained.

'What do you mean, "was"?' I asked.

'She was arrested and we never saw her again. She was one of the co-founders of an opposition group in favour of women's rights. She was tall, beautiful, sang like an angel and was the bravest person I have ever seen. She was adored by her followers, but to my younger sister and me, she was God.

'On the afternoon that she was arrested, the sky went black and wept until the early hours of the morning,' continued Claudia, 'and so did we.'

Claudia hid her face between her hands and cried. She cried as if she was eight years old again.

'What happened to you and your sister?' Turkan asked, desperately wanting her to stop crying.

'We were taken to our grandmother and she hid us for a few days in her flat. At the slightest noise, we hid under the bed and slept there during the nights. We lived in the dark while the curtains were drawn and we kept away from the windows. We spent most of the day sitting down, so that we wouldn't make unnecessary noise by walking. We didn't fight as sisters; actually, we hardly spoke or cried for our mum until we were smuggled out of Chile.' She sighed and paused to catch her breath.

'We sobbed for days when we arrived at our new home in Sweden. A Greek family took us in while we sought refuge in Sweden through the UN. We had some hard days, grieving for our mother's death, the loss of our motherland, our grandmother, family members and all that had been familiar and a home to us. We didn't even have a photo of our mother with us. Our shoes and the clothes on our body were our only belongings, the only souvenir of our past. The smell of Chile was soon washed out of our clothes, replaced with that of Swedish washing powder. We cried again and again until we had no more tears to cry.' She stopped.

I wanted to ask her to keep silent so that we could awake from her nightmare.

'You must be happy, living in safety?' Turkan asked, without much hope for a good ending to Claudia's story.

'I live with my sister and foster parents, who are kind to us both, and I am grateful for the life that I have been given. Believing in magic has been my saviour throughout my life and has been my strength,' she said, and winked at me.

'Listening to your story has made me want to believe in magic too,' I said, and thanked her.

Turkan and I walked silently towards the bus station. Sitting on the bus, we shed tears but wiped them from our cheeks, as though to deny the pain that Claudia's story had brought us. When we reached our flat, I could hear Shahin shouting as he argued with Mum.

'What is going on?' I asked, impatiently.

'I don't understand *why* I can't have two fathers!' Shahin was asking.

I looked at Mum and then at Turkan. With puffy eyes, she shrugged her shoulders.

I looked at Shahin and asked, 'What do you mean?'

'Patrik has two dads! He gets double of everything: Christmas gifts, birthday gifts, weekends away, summer holidays and treats, and they battle for his attention. Why can't I?'

'What do you mean, two dads? How can anyone have two dads?' Turkan asked, hoping to clarify the situation.

'One is his biological dad and the other one his stepdad,' Mum explained.

'Emil has three: one who is his biological father, one who is his younger brother's biological father and their new stepdad,' Shahin informed us.

We laughed until we were in tears.

Once we had laughed Claudia's story out of our systems, we went to the bedroom to find a very sulky Shahin.

'Some do not even have *one* father,' I said, thinking of Claudia.

'I don't want two or three dads; I just want my own back,' he cried under his duvet.

My mum hugged him and tried to comfort him with her words of wisdom and we heard the conversation move from longing, fear of loss and grief, into hope and love.

'You know, when I wanted to marry your dad, my mum told me, "All lovers have a god! If two people love each other equally passionately, the God of Love will bring them together and make them form a union of love." Sometimes when I miss your dad as much I do, I pray and send out messages to the God of Love, and ask for his mercy on me, who is so longing to be with your father. According to your grandmother, the God never disappoints,' my mum said, with a sigh.

On that note, while feeling the magic of love, we all held hands and prayed for my dad's safe arrival in the new land that we now called home.

SEVENTEEN

Whether it was the God of Love, the magic of Christmas or simply the Swedish government who had been working hard to grant my father a visa to enter the country, the day finally arrived when we could announce to our family and friends the date of his arrival.

Shahin filled the whole school with the joy of the news. Ulla was overwhelmed by the transformation in him. Mum was singing again as she cooked alongside Gulbahar and Turkan.

As for me, I kept my thoughts to myself. I didn't know how to feel; my dad coming meant that we were not returning, that the situation in Iran had not become any better but had got worse, that my maternal and paternal grandparents, my cousin and many more would be left on their own in a situation that everyone else was escaping from.

The Iraqi bombs filled the skies of Iran. People were emigrating, while those who stayed moved from city to city, trying to save what little life they owned. Inflation was truly high and the war had progressively reduced petrol and food rations.

Being so far away, longing to have my father with us but knowing that my extended family would lose their only support if he left them, was a guilt that I knew I had to live with. I had never felt so selfish in my life. Talking to Meme (my paternal grandmother), Maman Bozourg (my maternal grandmother) and the rest of my family briefly on the phone, I knew that they had to live through the pain but insisted that we should have my father with us in an unassailable country. Their selflessness made me feel even more guilty. I cried myself to sleep every night knowing that my grandparents would be struggling with their rations, queuing up for milk, petrol, oil, bread... In the past years they had lived through a revolution, war and the tragedies that were brought upon our nation, generation and motherland. I cried for their losses and further losses yet to come, when Dad would have to leave them behind.

A week before his arrival, while we were all struggling with our excitement, emotions and challenges ahead, Mum asked us to meet a new Swedish friend that she was proud to have made. She spoke non-stop about 'Bibbi Anderson', who was an expert on everything – everything we talked about and discussed was referred to Bibbi, which was short for Brigitta. She was a priest, a modern priest who was happily married with two beautiful daughters. To Mum this represented the 'perfect Swedish family home'. Bibbi loved Mum equally. Bibbi was the director of a Christian organisation where Mum used to seek refuge after her Swedish lessons at the adults' college, for help with her homework.

We were soon to call her *Moster* Bibbi (Auntie Bibbi); she was powerful in her community with such positive energy and lots of love to offer.

Bibbi was the first to hear of our great news and to celebrate it; she generously invited us over to her house for dinner. She lived in an eight-bedroom house in the countryside far away from the city, where she had to pick us up and drive for forty minutes in the dark and cold until we reached her beautiful home in the middle of nowhere. The house was cold so we had to make the fire, with the freshly cut wood in the fireplace. The smell of the fire brought back memories and put smiles on our faces.

'Can I watch some television?' Shahin asked.

'We don't own one!' Bibbi replied with a smile, hoping to reduce the pain of the disappointment with her big smile.

'No TV?' Shahin let out, disappointed but more feeling pity for the TV-less family.

'No TV! But you can help me in the kitchen, making dinner!' Bibbi offered with a bigger smile, as she disappeared into the kitchen.

'She hasn't made dinner yet and wants her guests to help her make it,' Shahin whispered to me.

It made me giggle.

'Come on,' I said. 'Let's go and learn how to make a Swedish meal!'

Shahin followed me into the kitchen, where we watched Bibbi and Mum whisking eggs and chopping spinach. We helped a bit with the salad and setting the table.

When the spinach omelette was made, we sat at the table. We said grace before dinner, and were offered a piece of omelette each, accompanied by a slice of homemade bread, salad and a choice of milk or water. The adults had a glass of wine.

'I'm still hungry,' Shahin whispered to me. His comment embarrassed me, even though I felt the same.

'We'll have homemade cookies with tea around the fire,' Bibbi announced, as if she had heard Shahin.

The homemade cookies sounded tempting and we were all inspired to help, clearing the table, washing the dishes and cleaning the kitchen, while the coffee was brewing and the aroma of homemade cookies filled the kitchen.

'One, two, three, four…' Bibi paused, counting the cookies while she dished them up. 'How many are we again?'

We looked at her with surprise until she realised that we were four people.

'What if someone wants to have two?' Shahin protested.

'True.' Bibi nodded and added one more cookie to the plate, half-smiling, pretty pleased with her gracious action.

Shahin and I burst out laughing and continued until Mum told us off. She tried to come up with an excuse to cover the reason for our laughter, while knowing exactly what we were laughing about.

While we were sitting by the hearth, feeling the heat from the fire, smelling the burning wood and nibbling the cookies to enjoy the sensation for as long as we could, Shahin asked if Bibbi could tell us a story.

'Once upon a time… (*En gång i tiden*),' Bibbi started, which put wide smiles on our faces, focused our attention and made our ears more attentive…

…there was a young girl called Agnes who helped her elderly father with the cattle and tried hard to fill her mother's empty space, taking care of her father and the household.

One afternoon, while she was driving the cattle home through the woods, she came to a high hill, and on the top of the hill, she saw a great manor. She felt so curious that she walked through the gates, leaving the cattle behind.

As she approached the manor, she enjoyed the garden, the flowers, the berry bushes and the wonderful fruit trees. When she reached it, she looked through the big old grey windows and saw a high table set with all sorts of food, cakes, pastries and fruit, which made her realise how hungry she was.

She held her rumbling tummy and walked through the big doors towards the dining room, aiming for the food on the table.

Suddenly, she heard a hiss and a whisper, and when she turned around, she saw a huge, handsome snake on a bed in the corner of the room.

The snake invited her to eat, to sit on the bed with him, but she found the snake too frightening and ran home.

The next day, when she woke up, her curiosity had returned and her dissatisfaction with her everyday life had increased. She decided to go in search of the hill, the manor house and the snake.

When she came to it and looked through the old grey windows, she saw that the same table was set, as if royalty were expected. The snake was lying there, as handsome as before, inviting her to eat and to sit by his side.

As soon as Agnes realised that the invitation from a charismatic, talking snake was indeed reality, she ran from the manor house and back to her cottage, as fast as her legs allowed her.

That evening, when she was having her supper at home, she looked at her slice of plain hard bread, with butter spread thinly on it, and thought of all that wonderful food – the fruit, cakes and sweets on the fancy dining table of the manor house – and suddenly she felt a breeze of courage, encouraging her to return to the manor.

Having struggled to make up her mind about what to do, at the fresh start of the next morning, she decided to make her way to the hill.

The long dining table was set, as tempting and glamorous as on the previous days. Agnes went slowly up to it and then walked around it, inhaling deeply the strong and sweet aroma of the roast ham, potatoes, carrots, fresh strawberries and cream, jelly, coloured sweets, and juicy seasonal fruits… until she came to the snake, who was staring at her.

'You are welcome to eat anything you wish on the table,' he said.

Agnes accepted the invitation and took a sweet. It tasted heavenly. The snake invited her to sit by his side. To her disbelief, Agnes did so. Then the snake asked her to kiss him.

Agnes looked into the snake's eyes. She became mesmerised by his charisma. She closed her eyes, moved forward towards the cheeks of the snake and kissed him. When she drew back and opened her eyes, she saw a very handsome prince sitting on the bed.

'I was hoping that you would be the one who would break the spell of the evil witch. I fell in love with you the moment you looked in at the window. So many girls have walked in, but they have all left, very frightened. The spell could only be broken by a brave girl who would kiss me, and I'm glad it was you!'

'This story is from Södermanland,' Bibbi continued. 'My mum used to tell it to us and I told it to my children, hoping that one day they would tell their children the same story.'

'Did they sleep well after you told them the story?' Shahin asked.

'*Hursâ* (why)?' asked Bibbi.

'It's not exactly a bed-time story!' Shahin said.

Mum elbowed him, Bibbi smiled and I bit my lip in embarrassment while we helped to make our beds. Shahin and I slept in the same room and bed as my mum, wondering if Bibbi would've found one of our folklore tales as interesting and weird as we found hers.

EIGHTEEN

It has been said that the Mughal emperor Shah Jahan caught a glimpse of the love of his life, Mumtaz Mahal, a Persian princess, hawking silk and glass beads. It was love at first sight and he wanted to marry her. He was fourteen and she was fifteen. It was five years before they married. In the year 1631, Mumtaz died in labour, giving birth to their fourteenth child.

On her deathbed, Shah Jahan promised never to remarry and vowed that he would build the richest mausoleum over her grave.

It is said that Shah Jahan was so heartbroken after her death that he ordered the court into mourning for two years. The Taj Mahal took twenty-four years and the labour of twenty-two thousand workers to construct. When Shah Jahan died, he was placed in a tomb, next to Mumtaz Mahal.

The Taj Mahal is a monument of love, symbolising the eternal love of a husband for his wife.

It's said that it was also love at first sight for my parents. They both described their love for each other as so overwhelming that they bounced between exhilaration, euphoria, increased energy, sleeplessness, loss of appetite, trembling and racing hearts; behaviour parallel to that of drug addicts.

According to researchers, love at first sight is not easy to explain, and some deny that it's even possible to fall profoundly in love after one quick glance. How can such a glance make us believe that we want to spend the rest of our lives in the arms of a stranger we have just seen for the first time?

Their love made such an impression on both of their families that the story of it was told, retold and continually referred to, from the day that it was created.

My father tells the story with such pride and boasts about the obstacles that their love had to overcome on its journey. He laughs when he tells the funny anecdote of how he asked their neighbour to call my mum's parents' house while he waited to take over the phone as soon as she picked up, to arrange dates with her; or the times when he hung around, in secret, outside the hospital, waiting for her to finish her shifts so he could give her a lift home.

Their journey to be wedded to each other was apparently an almost impossible mission to accomplish. Even today, when people hear about me being the daughter of Rostam and Shahla, they say, 'So you are the child of that love story!' To get permission to marry from both the families was apparently a curse that would only be broken by true love.

***

It was in the darkest month of the Swedish winter, when the day arrived for me to be reunited with my dad.

To look at my mum, it was like having a teenager with a crush in the flat. She laughed, she smiled, she got stressed over how perfect everything should be and should look. Gulbahar ran up and down from our flat to theirs, working alongside my mum. Turkan, Shahin and I stayed out of the way, while all the cooking, preparations and cleaning went on. We hid in one of the bedrooms in Turkan's flat downstairs.

'My dad will be so surprised by your Farsi,' I said to Turkan, really proud of her.

'Your dad will be really proud of you for your Swedish,' Turkan said, and smiled.

I looked at her with sisterly love. I had not known a friend like her before. I was grateful to the foreign motherland for giving me such a unique encounter, a love that I had not known before and such qualities within a person that I was in awe of and had learned from.

'You know, Turkan, you have been my rock during the time of our separation from my dad and our hardest days of adapting to a new country,' I said, meaning every word.

'You are my sister, my family, my country, my home,' she replied.

Shahin was mesmerised and shook his head in disbelief, saying, 'Love here, love there, love everywhere, today.'

We laughed. 'Will you come with us to pick my dad up from the airport?' he asked Turkan.

'I think that I can allow you one evening on your own as a family. I'll invade your home tomorrow morning.'

On that note, we went upstairs, got changed and, as a family of three, left to go to Arlanda Airport to welcome the head of our family who was rejoining us.

It was cold and dark and there was a thick layer of snow on the ground. It was clean, the cool air filled our lungs with its freshness and the lack of traffic was pleasant and felt calm.

I could barely wait for my dad to give us his first impressions of Sweden. I could barely wait for him to tell us about home, my grandparents, Ashkan, our house, how it was in Tehran and what the weather there was like.

I could barely wait to tell him about our best days and worst days, about our longing for our family back home, about our (mostly Mum's) sleepless nights, tears and heartache, about Shahin's and my way of adapting to the new family life without any directions of how to do it, about the weather and how to survive in the cold and...

I could barely wait to hug him and get that energy of a father's love that I had missed and gone without for the past year, to hear his voice properly without any interruptions or time limit.

I looked at Mum, and behind all those tears of joy, love and care for the arrival of my dad, who would at last be able to share the responsibility of parenthood with her, I noticed tears of sadness for the complete loss of connection to her home, family and loved ones. I sensed her fears, fear for my father's possible rejection of our new home, fear for his feelings about the new beginning in a frozen land far, and exceptionally different, from home. We all feared that.

Little did we know that this would be the beginning to a new chapter of life, in which he would learn and adapt fairly easily, study Swedish, find long-term Swedish friends, a decent job and fight hard for the Labour Party. He would have his favourite Swedish football team, while battling with his losses, blaming the West for the destruction of the East, for supplying weapons to support the war and

121

invasion by the Iraqis, blaming religion for the ignorance of the world, while educating the Swedes about Persia, its history and culture.

I remember the day as if it were yesterday. I will remember the moment of my parents' reunion until the last breath I take.

The glass wall at the Arlanda Airport arrival lounge was the only division between my parents now. He put one hand on his side of the glass and she put her hand on the other, and that moment of connection did not make me alone feel in awe of their love but also made the passengers, the cabin crews and the airport staff fascinated and tearful, while I could proudly hear the tune of their love-song in my head.

I silently prayed and wished for such love for myself.

Here he was! Truly here! He had escaped the war, the hardship, the fears and the land full of complications. He had arrived in a long khaki winter coat, long woollen navy trousers, a warm woollen beige sweater and a big Russian fur hat, leaving our loved ones behind in the hope of a new beginning in an unfamiliar part of the earth. He leaned on us to show him the way while chatting, laughing, smiling, touching our faces and telling us all about home.

'What are you wearing on your head, Dad?' Shahin asked, laughing.

We all laughed! He never wore that Russian hat again.

NINETEEN

It was a honeymoon period, being with my reunited family in our new home, a short distance away from our old flat and my darling Turkan, as we tried to adjust, adapt and learn to live as a whole family again in the city of Uppsala. We could finally see the beauty of Uppsala, capital city of Uppsala County, and appreciate the beautiful castle with its views of the botanical garden, the River Fyrisån that ran through the city and gave it life; but it was the old part of the city, Gamla Uppsala, with its history of the arrival of Christianity and the end of the regular sacrificial rites, that fascinated us the most.

As soon as my dad bought a car we explored Uppsala and discovered other cities of Sweden, near and far. We saw our new life in a different light.

Mum seemed more relaxed; she slept better and smiled more, and studied for her nursing exam. Shahin was happier; he felt supported by my dad's presence and regained his good humour. I enjoyed the day that had finally arrived, when we became a family again. Our very own Turkan cycled over, if not every day, at least every other day, to see us, have tea and practise her Farsi.

One afternoon when Turkan had come to visit, Mum had gone to the communal laundry room while Dad was organising our outdoor storage, Shahin, Turkan and I decided to entertain ourselves, cooking. We made dough from scratch and Turkan now taught us how to make the filling for *kömbe* (Turkish pastries) from scratch too, with chicken, onions and spices.

'What's that smell? It smells heavenly!' my dad said, when he opened the door.

'We're making *kömbe*,' Shahin said enthusiastically.

'Look what I found!' Dad said with even more enthusiasm in his voice, holding up a letter.

We all stared at the mysterious letter in his hand, until he explained. 'Your Maman Bozourg asked me to deliver this story to you. She said that it was one that she had never told before and thought that it would be the best gift I could bring you from her. I just found it in the pocket of the suitcase while I was clearing the storage,' he said, smiling.

We looked at the letter as if he was holding on to treasure, with astonishment and pride. Proud to know such an incredible soul, who had once again found her way across oceans, rivers and mountains to reach us and remain with us for ever through her teachings about life, via her immortal tales.

I had never felt happier, being surrounded by love from my reunited family and an additional family member in our new home in a foster motherland. I felt hopeful about our new life while I listened peacefully to one of Maman Bozourg's stories.

'Once upon a time…' I read aloud, with tears in my eyes and a lump in my throat.

Zaal: a treasure from the *Shahnameh*, the great *Book of Kings*, by Ferdousi

...When people remember Zaal, they think of his white hair that shone like silver, his powerful physique that was built during his challenging years in the Alborz Mountains, so that he was able to survive after he had been abandoned by his father, the great King Saam, or his upbringing by the amazing Simurgh, the bird with feathers of a thousand colours, but his love story is rarely spoken of. This love story, culminating in the birth of his son, Rostam, the great warrior, made the history of Persia complete.

The story goes that after Zaal's return to his father's palace, he lived as a prince, indulged in luxury, comfort and beauty. King Saam ensured that he lived up to his vow of making Zaal the happiest prince of all times.

One day Zaal decided to explore the east and, with his father's permission, he travelled with his adviser and teacher to Kabul. The King of Kabul, Mehraab, greeted the Prince generously with gifts, and impressed him with his kind spirit.

Word reached Zaal that he should accept dinner at the palace with the King and his family, to meet Princess Rudabeh, who was more radiant than the sun, with hair as black as the night sky, lips as red as cherries and eyes as golden as the narcissus in spring, with eyebrows that arched like a rainbow, raven-black lashes and hair that smelled like orange blossom.

That night Zaal did not sleep. He was in already love! He had fallen in love with the idea of the mesmerising princess, but he knew that he could not accept the King's invitation to dinner, as he was not allowed by his father to dine with people who did not believe in God.

At the palace, King Mehraab told his wife and daughter about the Prince, and awakened Rudabeh's curiosity. That same evening, Rudabeh called for her chambermaids and devised a cunning plan.

Her loyal maids followed her instructions carefully and made sure that Zaal and his men overheard their conversation, praising Rudabeh's beauty, kindness and wisdom.

Zaal was determined to meet the Princess and asked the maids to bring him secretly to see her. They led him to the tower, where Rudabeh was waiting at the window.

It only took one look exchanged between them before they both knew their reason for being born. With hearts beating quickly and stammering words, they declared their love for one another and made vows to stay true.

Zaal rode back to persuade his father, reminding him of the promise he had made on Mount Alborz to make his son the happiest prince alive, if only he would leave Simurgh and return to his father's kingdom.

King Saam listened attentively to Zaal's request and wholeheartedly felt his son's passionate love for Rudabeh but couldn't help feeling concerned for his country's safety. He set out to visit King Mehraab, to consult him about the matter. In the meantime, Mehraab had been confronted by his wife Sindukht about Zaal. She hadn't expected Mehraab's reaction.

'How dare she ask me to put my kingdom, my rule and my success at risk?' he yelled. 'Bring her to me so I can have her killed for the future of Kabul!'

Sindukht begged him to have mercy on her only daughter. 'Please don't do anything you'll regret. There must be a better solution. I will sit with you until we find one,' she pleaded.

In the meantime, Zaal, who had ridden and reached his father that afternoon, dismounted from his horse, kissed the ground before his father's feet, and spoke. 'In your land you're known for your fairness and honesty, but I have received nothing but injustice from you. You abandoned me as child, sent me to the mountains and left me to be eaten by the wolves, but when you found me, in your regret you promised to fulfil my every desire. My happiness lies with Rudabeh. If I cannot have her, then end my misery and kill me now. I cannot live without her.'

On these words, Saam's eyes filled with tears and he embraced Zaal. He wrote a letter to Shah Manouchehr, the great Emperor of Persia, who was also against the marriage of Zaal and Rudabeh. King Saam believed that the kingdoms would be put in jeopardy by their marriage. He believed Rudabeh's ancestors traced back to the evil King Zahhak, which would raise concern in the people of both lands.

Zaal was greeted gracefully by Shah Manouchehr, who listened to his words and then read the letter from his father, asking the Shah to reconsider his decision.

'I, Saam e Nariman, have given nothing but sadness and pain to my son Zaal throughout his life, and the one thing that he asks of me that would make him happy lies in your hands. I ask of you to allow me to give permission and my blessings for their marriage, so that I can fulfil his only request of me.'

127

Impressed by the great King Saam's words, feeling sympathetic yet apprehensive for the state, Shah Manouchehr called for his astrologers, and asked what lay in store for Zaal and Rudabeh in the future. Their words were quite positive and predicted a good marriage, a good life and also a beneficial connection for Iran.

Shah Manouchehr was still not completely convinced, so he asked his wise men to test Zaal on his intelligence. Zaal would replace Saam one day, and the Shah wanted to be confident about this replacement.

His men tested Zaal by asking him five riddles:

There are twelve evergreens, and each has about thirty branches. What are they?

There are two valuable and fast horses. One horse is black and the other one is white. These horses chase each other but can never catch each other, no matter how fast they run or how hard they try. How can this be?

There are roughly thirty riders. One passes, thirty still remain. Why?

There is a field, and in this field, a strong man takes the life of the living, young and old, with a machete. Who is he?

There is a lovely town on top of a mountain, but the townspeople leave it one by one and head towards the desert. A tragedy occurs, and that causes these people to return one by one to the lovely town. What is happening?

Zaal thought in silence for a long while, and eventually he said, 'The twelve evergreens are the twelve months of the year, and their branches are the thirty days in each month. The black horse is night and the white horse is day. The thirty riders are the thirty days of a month. When one day passes in the calendar, all the days in the month still remain. The man with the machete is time, the lovely town represents heaven and the desert is earth. All the living come to earth but return to heaven when they die.'

Shah Manouchehr was utterly impressed and inspired by Zaal's intelligence, and blessed his union with Rudabeh. He wrote a letter to King Saam, in which he thanked Saam for his loyalty over the years and granted permission for Zaal to marry Rudabeh.

On the other side of the country, King Saam had decided to ride to Kabul and meet the royal family. When the news reached King Mehraab, he assumed that Saam had come with the intention of killing him. Mehraab called for his wife and once again yelled that she and Rudabeh had destroyed his pride, his kingdom and the future of his land.

'First I will kill you and then your daughter,' he stormed.

Sindukht once again managed to calm her husband, by suggesting that she should meet King Saam on her own and take away the tension.

When she met King Saam, she brought jewellery to bestow upon him and greeted him pleasantly. But the king was not pleased by this greeting. He wondered about the reason for this royal lady to receive him instead of King Mehraab himself. He was not impressed by the jewellery and lacked understanding of her behaviour.

'Please reveal your true identity to me, and, as you must be close to the king, please tell me how Zaal met Shahzadeh Rudabeh. I find it strange that a king would send a lady to receive me,' Saam said firmly.

'I am Sindukht, wife of King Mehraab and mother of Rudabeh. Rudabeh is in love with your son and is willing to give up her life for him. However I am not prepared to allow their love to cause a war between Iran and Kabul, which would take the lives of many innocent people,' she explained. Then she went on to tell the warrior king about how Zaal and Rudabeh met.

'I agree that their love should bring prosperity to the lands and not war and bloodshed.' He nodded. 'I admire your honesty and bravery, and hope to see these qualities in Rudabeh too. I shall add my own to Shah Manouchehr's blessing on their union in marriage.'

Saam returned home and, on his arrival, Zaal greeted him with a letter from King Manouchehr. A weight had been lifted off Sam's shoulders and he was proud to finally have brought his son joy and made his wish reality. Saam immediately sent a group of men to Kabul to bring King Mehraab the good news.

Their union was finally blessed and happy days arrived for the soulmates when the long-awaited wedding was celebrated in Kabul.

Soon after the wedding night Rudabeh became pregnant. She had a difficult pregnancy and the baby could not be delivered, as it had grown so big. Rostam e Pahlevan, the hero of all times in the great *Book of Shahnameh*, was the son born to Zaal and Rudabeh.

Her pain was so great that in the end she lost consciousness. In his desperation, Zaal remembered Simurgh's promise. He set fire to her feather and asked for help.

'I am losing the love of my life. Almighty God is witness to all my tears, prayers, struggles and sacrifices to be with her. I cannot live without her. Please spare her for me, Simurgh. I'll do anything to save her.'

Simurgh told Zaal to stay strong and to concentrate. She suggested that the baby could be delivered from Rudabeh's body by cutting her belly. Then Simurgh offered him a remedy to smear over the wound, to make it heal.

Before she left she gave him one more feather to call her next time he was in need.

In this way the great hero Rostam e Pahlevan was born to his joyful parents, Zaal and Rudabeh.

Left with the message that 'love overcomes all obstacles', we enjoyed our freshly baked *kömbe*, dreaming of the bright future and silently promising to aim for the best as a loving family in this new land.

TWENTY

Solvej is a personification of the expression 'One in a million'. She is the loveliest, kindest, most adorable Swedish lady we have had the honour to know. She came to us to prove that kindness has nothing to do with the colour of your skin. She was, and will always remain, the guardian angel of our family.

No birthday had passed without us having had an acknowledgement from her; there had been no difficult day without her being at my mum's side; not a tear had been shed without Solvej offering her shoulder to be cried on; no accomplishment or achievement happened without Solvej being involved in the process. Solvej, my Swedish aunt, stood by Mum for better or worse, for richer or poorer, in sickness and in health, until at last death did them part.

'Can you open the door, Shirin?' my dad asked.

We knew that it was Solvej. I recognised her calm and gentle footsteps up to the front door, her considerate knocking as she waited patiently at the door.

Her hug warmed my heart.

'How is he?' she asked.

'Worse than yesterday,' I replied. I felt exhausted.

'It'll get better with time,' she said confidently.

Unable to believe her, I shrugged my shoulders and would not meet her eye.

'Are you done packing?' she asked.

'As much as I possibly could. He wouldn't let me. I would pack her clothes in the boxes and he would unpack them, growling and wailing, sobbing over the clothes, not letting go.'

Solvej shed a tear. 'Time will heal,' she said in a lower voice but this time sounding only half-convinced, as if she needed to believe that it would.

I said nothing.

'Can you help me with the boxes downstairs? We'll load my car so your dad doesn't have to drive,' she said.

I showed Solvej the stacked-up boxes.

'They smell of Mum,' I whispered.

I wiped my tears.

When in the car, my dad looked out of the front passenger window, I looked out of the left back passenger window while the windscreen belonged to Solvej. She seemed to focus on the road and concentrate on the directions that had been carefully worked out on a piece of paper.

'We are not far,' Solvej said, as if she wanted to break the silence. 'I was on a course last week and the subject was empathy, and I thought of you two. May I tell you a story?'

Both my dad and I were known for being big fans of folktales and strong believers in them, but we still said nothing, as if nothing meant anything anymore. We were grief-stricken, and there was no meaning or sense in the world around us.

Solvej chose to tell the story.

133

Once upon a time there was a beautiful young bird with colourful feathers. She enjoyed life and wanted to explore and get to know as much of it as she could.

She was passionate about nature and fascinated by its beauty. She was playful and curious about life, even when sometimes it seemed to be to her disadvantage. She loved to hide in the bushes and make noises to scare the passers-by. She also liked to play hide and seek with the other birds. She enjoyed playing 'catch me if you can' with the squirrel.

She liked to build her nest in one of the strongest and biggest, and probably oldest, trees in the area. She felt safe and protected by the broad leaves of the tree. She felt at home.

One day the bird noticed some changes, not only in the weather but also in the colours of nature. She was again fascinated by this and wanted to learn more and as much as possible. Soon she realised that she had to deal with the disappearance of what had been lost in order to be able to make room for the new.

The changes continued, not for the better but for the worse, in the bird's eyes. Each day there were changes in the colour of the leaves, from yellow to orange, and by the time it had reached brown the bird had become very worried.

When she saw the other birds and creatures leaving she felt that her tree particularly had become ill. It must be ill because of the cold, she decided. She also decided to stay and keep the tree company; this was the least she could do to prove that she cared for it.

The tree started to lose its brown leaves one by one, and became balder and balder every day. The bird was very upset to witness this. She found it difficult to undergo this process along with the tree. She felt that she hadn't given the tree enough help for it to recover from its illness.

She felt cold, powerless and in pain, like the tree. Soon bald patches started to appear on her wings. When she took a closer look at herself, she realised that in the process of sharing the tree's pain she was also losing her beautiful and colourful feathers.

As the tree became balder and balder so did the bird, until finally both were quite naked.

The days gradually became longer, the colours gradually returned and the great strong tree gradually regained its big beautiful green leaves, while the bird perched on that tree, naked and cold.

'There is nothing wrong with grieving, in fact it is a necessity, but remember not to get stuck in the process,' Solvej added, with a brief smile.

My whole Swedish life flashed before my eyes as I looked out of the window. The day my mum was awarded her nursing certificate in Swedish, my dad's fiftieth birthday, when he was celebrated by his colleagues at the hospital, the day Shahin announced his engagement, the day I held Turkan's first-born and finally, the day I left my adoptive motherland to make a new home with my husband in Britain.

Comfortably lost in the past, I heard Solvej say, 'Oh, there it is!', trying to catch my eye in the mirror, pointing at the most impressive cathedral I had ever seen. It looked majestic and spiritual, with a rainbow arching over the holy monument.

Solvej stepped out of the car and opened the doors for us too. I felt mesmerised by the cathedral's beauty and holiness.

A strange and serene calm surrounded the three of us. The warmth of the sacred place held us and it felt good, as we waited for the nuns to open the door. It was an unusually long wait, as if we were being assessed before being admitted. But the wait did not feel uncomfortable.

The door opened ajar. We saw the eye of a nun peering out and heard her say, 'Can I help you?'

'We are here to deliver some goods as required in my mum's will. She asked me to...' I said, trying to make eye contact with her before explaining more.

'Oh my Lord!' she cried, and let go of the door. 'Shahla is here!'

At that point other nuns hurried to the door, children ran up while their parents tried to pull them back. With support from Solvej, I explained that I was Shahla's daughter, while at the same time trying to pick up my heavily tranquillised, grieving dad from the doorstep, where he had fallen, heartbroken, on his knees again.

They invited us in and offered us tea and sweets.

'These are made by Zeynab, one of the asylum seekers who lives here,' one nun said, and pointed at the date pastries. Zeynab came to sit with us and gave us the recipe for them, while obviously appreciating the sight of us enjoying them. She explained in the rather good Swedish that she had learned there that she was one of many illegal asylum seekers who had been rejected by the government. The support of Queen Silvia had enabled the chapel to remain free from the authorities, who were under no circumstances allowed to enter the building unless the nuns voluntarily let them in. This meant that they needed everything they could get in the way of medicine, food, clothes, beddings, medical and psychological support, and so forth.

'Once a month Shahla would visit us with food, giving us support and her precious time. I wish I could say something to ease your pain, but I cannot find any words. I feel her loss too,' Sister Magdalena said, and closed her eyes.

Solvej and I brought in the boxes, full mainly of Mum's clothes and shoes, some unworn and some used. The nuns opened the boxes while the children took out the clothes, hats and shoes and played dressing-up. It made me smile to see so many happy faces.

Sister Magdalena stamped on the floor three times before a door to the underground passage opened and out climbed girls, who then chose clothes and shoes. The atmosphere was phenomenal. So much joy suddenly surrounded us, while Sister Magdalena hummed a hymn. It felt soothing to our damaged souls.

'Shahla has managed once again to bring us all joy and laughter, even from the other side. Only she would be capable of doing that. People with great souls do not die,' Sister Magdalena said to me at the doorstep. 'These are my only words of comfort for you, my child: be blessed and walk with peace, like your mother.'

We never returned.

May the best of blessings come to the person who gives blessings to others.

O wise one, may your knowledge grow throughout the days of your long life of joy, through your most advanced mentality, the wondrous wisdom of your good mind, which you developed by means of righteousness.

– Zarathustra

EPILOGUE

When I feel blocked in my thoughts, when I am mired in grief and losing my religion, I think of the life of the Messenger of Unseen Power.

One horrible day, when my face was filled with hormonal pimples, I had cramps in my lower back and my belly felt double its size, I was craving sweets and had a slight headache and my hair looked wild, I found an empty spot on a bench at lunch time in the school yard, feeling sorry for myself and wanting to hide away my new-found monstrous being – I was hitting puberty.

'Are you sunbathing?'

There he was, the mystery guy who always kept himself to himself, who had only recently joined senior school for extra Swedish tuition, always wore a hoodie and never smiled.

I looked up and wondered where the sun to be bathing in might be, but instead I asked, with irritation, 'Am I taking your spot?', thinking that he of all people must understand the need for privacy.

'I see! Is it that time of the month?'

'No!' I yelled, wondering what must have given it away.

'Oh, so you're always this moody then?' he asked, with a cheeky smile on his face.

My eyes were ready to pop out of my head at his comment but, with my jaw clenched, I snarled, 'How rude!'

Realising that he must've pushed me a little too far, he sat next to me before I had a chance to stand up and leave, lowered his head and whispered, 'I have two sisters back home in Shiraz, so I'm familiar with the condition.'

After a few deep breaths to cool myself down, I broke the silence, trying to sound reasonable. 'You must miss them,' I said.

'If only you knew,' he said, almost interrupting me. 'Today is my eighteenth birthday,' he said, looking at me.

I looked up into his deep brown eyes and saw more than I had asked for. I recognised the pain, the longing, the loss, the loneliness and the hardship of adjustment to this new motherland.

'From today, I am officially allowed to live on my own. I have been living with my Swedish foster family since my arrival.'

He opened his arms in a grateful gesture to the universe, calling out, 'Yes to no more peeling and eating potatoes, no more having milk as a drink with dinner, and best of all, no more hiding in my room and apologising to the son of the household for sharing his space and for becoming the perfect son that his parents had always wished for. No more hearing the weeping of his mother in the middle of the night, as she is rejected by her husband. No more having to be a witness to the binge-drinking of the "failed" father of the family. And finally, no more knocks on my bedroom door, during the night, the daughter of the family asking if I'm asleep.'

My heart ached for him. I didn't dare look up in case he saw my tears.

'Don't worry, I barricade my bedroom door with the desk before I go to bed,' he whispered, lowering his face again. 'This is the best day since the day of my arrival. Today is the day I have been waiting for; it is the day that will reward all my hardship and pay for all my hard work. When I look back, I can tell my children, your dad climbed mountains, rode on horses, slept on nothing but bare rocks in the freezing cold, in the most inhuman circumstances, to get to my destination, which starts today, 12th March '86.

'I'll especially tell them the funny story of how I was stopped at the airport in Turkey by a police officer, looking at my Swedish fake passport, before I boarded the flight,' he continued. 'When I insisted that I was Swedish, they told me to speak Swedish to a Swedish passenger standing in line. The passenger was kind enough to ask me closed questions, to which all I had to do was reply "*Ja*" or "*Nej*"! Once on the plane, I told him some of my story about "being the victim of injustice in my world as a young adolescent". On arrival, he gave me his business card and told me to get in touch if I ever needed help. I haven't felt the need to, yet.'

I felt warm on that chilly day but said nothing. I half-smiled at the hero with whom I had had the privilege of sharing the best day of his life.

'The name is Arshia, by the way,' he said. As he stood up to leave, he continued, 'I'll see you tomorrow, by which time I will be eighteen and you will be feeling much better, I'm sure!

I hugged my tummy and, feeling slightly embarrassed, said, 'See you tomorrow!'

In the evening, I felt a change in me; I felt more grateful for my destiny, thankful to the universe and positive about my future. I had been made to think about the human survival instinct, heroism and the mysterious ways in which the universe acts. I fell asleep after writing a mental thank-you note to everyone and everything for being such a precious part of my life.

When Arshia's death was announced in the assembly the following morning, my thank-you note was torn into thousand pieces.

Apparently, after getting off the bus and crossing in front of it, he didn't see the car which was passing the bus at high speed. I was told that he hadn't suffered and had died instantly.

***

With time I have learned to feel blessed by such deep lessons, which I have received from tragic experiences, as I have realised that the universe would endow me with the courage and grace to face hardships. I eventually learned to be grateful to that hero in spirit, Arshia, who redirected me through his life story, giving me a message that transformed me: 'Be grateful for today, and never take anything for granted. Life is a blessing.'

ABOUT THE AUTHOR

Shirin Amani Azari is an Iranian-born Swedish mother of a thirteen-year-old daughter. She lives with her family in Kent, working as a psychotherapist during the day, while pursuing her great passion for writing at the same time.

At the age of twelve she left Iran and has never returned. Her Swedish life began in the city of Uppsala, where she lived until a year before she emigrated with her husband to London in 1997.

Her first book, *Once Upon a Time in Tehran*, was published in New York in 2009. This proved to be a success through various book signings in New York and London, one of which, at Harrods, had a great turn-out. She was also interviewed by the three most-viewed Iranian television companies in England and USA; *Tapesh*, *Manoto TV* and her recent interview was with *Sina Valiollah* on *MBC Persia*. She won awards from the BBC Persian Service and had a further book signing in New York in 2010. *Once Upon a Time in Tehran* was published in both hard and soft cover.

Once Upon a Time in Uppsala was written with the hope of raising awareness of an immigrant life as seen through the eyes of a twelve-year-old child. The author's intention is to help other children in the same situation, children who are silently suffering in a world where hostility to immigrants and refugees is growing, to find their own voice, which will aid their integration into society.

Shirin is committed to her charitable work, in which she is a strong believer. She offers her services to the Medical Alliance for Health Services Abroad (MAHSA), believing in the future of young people in Iran.

Restoring stories such as tales from Persian folklore is a passion for her, and she has referred to this in both her books. She believes that a story can tell us more than any academic lecture. Tales create magic and wonder, and teach us about life, ourselves and others.

Her previous writing experiences include articles published in the *International Journal of Psychotherapy* and *The Therapist*, amongst other journals in the field of her profession.

Website: shirinamaniazari.com
E-mail: shirinazari@ntlworld.com